INSIDE THE MIND
OF A GODLY HUSBAND

INSIDE THE MIND

OF A GODLY HUSBAND

His Beliefs, His Thoughts, His Growth.

GENE REDD

Inside the Mind of a Godly Husband
Copyright © 2013 by Gene Redd

ISBN-13: 978-0615871837
ISBN-10: 0615871836

Library of Congress Control Number: 2013916147

Unless otherwise noted, Scripture quotations are from the Holy Bible: New International Version®. © 1973, 1978, 1984 by the International Bible Society. Used by permission of Zondervan Publishing House. All rights reserved.

Scripture quotations marked KJV are from the Holy Bible, King James Version.

Scripture quotations marked NASB are from the New American Standard Bible®, © by The Lockman Foundation 1960, 1962, 1963, 1968, 1971, 1972, 1973, 1975, 1977, 1995. Used by permission.

Scripture quotations marked NLT are from the Holy Bible, New Living Translation. © 1996. Used by permission of Tyndale House Publishers, Inc.,Wheaton, Illinois 60189. All rights reserved.

Scripture quotations marked AMP are from the Amplified® Bible, © 1954, 1958, 1962, 1964, 1965, 1987 by The Lockman Foundation. Used by permission. (www.Lockman.org)

Scripture quotations marked (CEV) are from the Contemporary English Version Copyright © 1991, 1992, 1995 by American Bible Society, Used by Permission.

Contents

Introduction

Inside The Mind of a Godly Husband (ITMOAGH) is a book that explores the mindset and character of God as demonstrated within the life of a husband. The book examines the process by which a man becomes "godly," from the moment he is introduced to Jesus Christ, all the way up to the point of his maturation.

ITMOAGH describes how a man extracts essential fruit from his marriage to Jesus Christ, in order to effectively meet the needs of his wife. The book highlights the leadership traits of love, responsibility, oneness, and vision, and provides practical examples of how husbands reveal these traits on a day-to-day basis.

ITMOAGH is comprised of ten easy-to-read chapters, all of which have been outlined and summarized below for your convenience.

Chapter 1: **"A Husband's Death."** This chapter addresses man's perpetual fear of death, and how it affects every aspect of his life. It also examines the legacy of death passed down by Adam and how a man's spiritual heritage positions him to overcome this.

<u>Chapter 2</u>: **"A Husband's Walk with God."** This chapter looks at the formation of the husband's relationship with Christ and unveils the very intricate process of deliverance. The chapter also highlights the very important distinction between a man's spirit, the Holy Spirit, and sinful nature.

<u>Chapter 3</u>: **"A Husband's Personal Responsibility."** This chapter highlights the importance of "ownership" as the central piece of the husband's willingness to accept responsibility. It focuses on the three essential traits of responsibility, and how each plays a respective role in the overall landscape of ownership.

<u>Chapter 4</u>: **"A Husband's Godly Responsibility."** This chapter examines the husband's greatest responsibility, and how this one responsibility translates into all the other subsequent responsibilities that a man has unto his neighbor. The chapter also highlights seven of these responsibilities and explains how the husband goes about fulfilling them each and every day.

<u>Chapter 5</u>: **"A Husband's Marriage Responsibility."** This chapter examines the significance of the husband's leadership role within the marriage union. It explains the seven fundamental marriage responsibilities that a husband has, and ties in eleven principles to help the husband in fleshing out his unique leadership position.

<u>Chapter 6</u>: **"A Husband's Oneness."** This chapter focuses on

the purpose of oneness and how God brings a husband and wife together. It also outlines eleven critical areas that a man must focus on in order to successfully unite with his wife.

<u>Chapter 7</u>: "A Husband's Vision." This chapter examines the three types of vision that a godly husband uses to assess and respond to his family's needs. Each of these vision types plays a unique and critical role in how a godly husband sets the strategic direction for his family.

<u>Chapter 8</u>: "A Husband's Scriptures." This chapter highlights the godly husband's 24 most powerful scriptural discoveries, and places specific emphasis on critical values such as identity in Christ, faith, family, and personal responsibility.

<u>Chapter 9</u>: "A Husband's Devotional." This chapter contains over 50 principles with accompanying scriptures for meditation and contemplation. It covers a broad range of topics, and delivers extremely powerful insights for the godly husband.

<u>Chapter 10</u>: "A Husband's Notes." This chapter offers a vast assortment of quick, bulleted, step-by-step processes in order to help the godly husband achieve a healthy, prosperous, marriage to the Lord.

ITMOAGH is truly a transformative piece that redefines the way a husband looks at marriage. It takes timeless biblical fundamentals for Christ-Centered relationships and converts them into practical advice for everyday living. I pray that your life is blessed by this book in the same way it has blessed mine.

Get ready for the journey!

Gene Redd

Chapter 1

A Husband's Death

A Husband Must Confront His Fear of Death

"..And also that he might deliver and completely set free all those who through the haunting fear of death were held in bondage throughout the whole course of their lives."

Hebrews 2:15-16 (AMP)

"Everyone Wants To Live"

Whether it's his life, his family, his car, his home, his money, or simply his place in line, man is deathly afraid of losing. He fears loss of anything and everything. He even panics when he loses his train of thought. He struggles with loss because it symbolizes death to him. And no man wants to die, every man wants to live. Even the martyr takes his own life with the warped expectation that he'll have a better afterlife because of his valiant actions. The confused teenager takes his life to experience a life free from pain and disappointment. Each and every day, some man, somewhere on the planet, attempts to kill himself, not because he wants to die, but because he wants to live.

"Pursuing Life vs The Fight To Stay Alive"

Every man wants to live, but not every man wants to pursue life. Sadly, most men spend their limited time on this earth fighting to stay alive. And there's a big difference between a man who pursues life and a man who fights to stay alive. For the man who fights to stay alive, "self-preservation" is the primary end goal. His life revolves around protecting himself from life's hurts, pains, and disappointments. He desperately wants to experience life, but the fear of death paralyzes any and all attempts to pursue it. As a result, this man enlists himself in a lifelong campaign to stay alive at any expense.

The man who pursues life sees things from a much different perspective. This man focuses on "the giving of self" as a primary means to life. He's motivated by the joy that springs from his obedience to Christ, and challenges himself to love others in ways that increase his faith. He makes decisions, based not upon what he'll gain in the end, but rather, whether the end will bring him closer to Christ. The man who pursues life has no need to enlist in the fight to stay alive.

"How a Man Fights To Stay Alive"

A man fights to stay alive in very subtle ways. Sometimes he does it by pointing out the flaws in other people; sometimes he does it by lashing out in anger; sometimes he does it by spewing insults or gossiping. When a man does these types things, he tells the entire world that he's fighting to stay alive.

A man's fight to stay alive is often disguised among the most common of behaviors:

> **A man fights to stay by avoiding doctors** (because he fears the death that comes by way of a bad diagnosis).

> **A man fights to stay alive by overeating** (because he fears the death that comes by way of hunger).

> **A man fights to stay alive by dying his hair or getting a toupee** (because he fears the death that comes by way of becoming old and unattractive).

> **A man fights to stay alive by cutting lines** (because he fears the death that comes by way of falling behind).

> **A man fights to stay alive by becoming aggressive** (because he fears the death that comes by way of losing control).

Seldom do we take the time to examine the motivations behind these types of behaviors. But the truth is, each day, man fleshes out his insatiable fight to stay alive, driven by his unrelenting fear of death.

"Living Out The Fear of Death"

The man who fights to stay alive is living proof that the fear of death pervades his way of thinking. But despite his condition, this man still has difficulties understanding the connection between his fears and his actions. So he'll behave in certain ways, unaware of the fact that his behavior stems from his underlying fear of death. He'll procrastinate and avoid household chores, unbeknownst to the fact that he does these things because he's afraid to die. He'll grab the biggest meal portion for himself at dinner without a hint of consideration for anyone else around him. Most would indict such a man without hesitation; completely unaware that behind his behavior is a constant prodding in his heart that tells him, "You'll die if you don't get the best part for yourself."

Some men are plagued with patterns of yelling, threatening, manipulating, and even hitting their wives. These situations are absolutely tragic, and in most circumstances, criminal. But what's even more tragic is the fact that the deep-rooted fear of death that accompanies such behavior often goes undetected. **A man's fight to stay alive is the odorless, colorless, fear-driven toxin that subtly invades his body without him even knowing it.**

"Man's Death Legacy"

When the first man (Adam) ate of the forbidden fruit in the Garden, it was an act of disobedience that brought death, sickness and disease into the world. Through one single act, death gained dominion over man. This left man with no other choice than to live his entire life "in bondage, haunted by the fear of death" as described in Hebrews 2:15. Ever since then, man has walked the earth engulfed by a prison of fear, marked by insecurities, paranoia's, and struggles to find his true identity. This is the death legacy passed down from Adam.

"How Man Overcame the Legacy of Death"

When Jesus Christ died on the cross, the death sentence that once loomed over man finally was repealed. This removed death's legal power and dominion over man. And with death no longer occupying legal power and dominion over man, man no longer needed to fear death. Therefore, for the man who is "born again" (born of the Spirit of Christ), he can rest assured in knowing that the power of death that once plagued him finally has been overcome.

"Death and the Christian"

I would love to report that Christians no longer struggle with the fear of death or death-related issues; but of course, that is not the case. Many Christians, though spiritually redeemed and made anew in Christ, still walk in that remnant of fear, which for thousands of years was interwoven into the fabric of humanity. Before Christ, fear permeated every aspect of man's being, from how he related to God, all the way down to how he related to people (even himself). But Jesus took away man's "life of fear" and substituted it with "a life of faith." That's what Christians call "the good news." The "not so good news" is that the obsession with fear that once dominated man for so many years didn't depart from him so quickly.

Unfortunately, for many Christians, the fear of death still holds the same power that it had over them when they were in bondage to the law of sin and death. As a result, we see Christians in the world today living lives dominated by the fear of death. We see Christians living lives dominated by the fear of unhappiness. We see Christians living lives dominated by the fear of hurt. We see Christians living lives dominated by the fear of loneliness. All of these fears are sourced from man's central and most prolific fear; the fear of death. In many ways, the fear of death is just as prevalent within the life of the today's Christian as it is the non-Christian. From a Christian public relations perspective, this is absolutely devastating.

"Self Rules the World"

The world lives according to what is called "the self-principle." The self-principle is a life philosophy that first and foremost focuses on the preservation of self. Because of man's incessant fear of death, he'll try to keep himself alive at any expense. And if ever his life is threatened, he'll step on, hurt, maim, or even kill another person in order to stay alive.

The self-principle dictates that the worst inside of a man will come out of him if ever his life is threatened. So if criticism resides deep inside of a man, criticism will be fiercely unleashed if ever his life is threatened. If spite resides deep inside of a man, spite will be venomously released if ever his life is threatened. If anger resides deep inside of a man, anger will be violently released if ever his life is threatened. The self-principle brings out the worst inside of a man when confronted with the possibility of death. Why else would a man kill another man simply because of a disrespectful look? Why else would two men fight to the death simply because of an accidental bumping of shoulders? **It's a man's combustible, deep-seeded, fear of death that ushers him into conflict with the world.**

Have you ever encountered someone in your life that you thought was simply "out to get you?" It may have been a coworker, a neighbor, or maybe even a business associate or a family member. In your mind, you were convinced that this person was put on the earth for no other reason than to give you misery. Well, I have good news for you. That person wasn't put in your life to give you misery. Nor did that person treat you the way they did because they disliked you, hated you, or wanted to see you destroyed. That person treated you the way that they did because you (in some way) posed a very real threat to their life. And as a result, that person lived out the self-principle, doing whatever they could to try and keep themselves alive at your expense.

The self-principle makes a man humiliate others out of his own fear of being humiliated. It makes a man to tell jokes about others out of his own fear of being made fun of. It makes a man insult others out of his own fear of being insulted. The self-principle makes a man believe that he'll feel better about himself by exposing the weaknesses of others. Whenever a man finds himself mistreated, he should not be quick to personalize his offense. The chances are, his offender is being driven by the self principle, and in some way feels as if his life is threatened.

The first thing you should do when confronting someone who is threatened by you is help that person understand that you are no threat to their life. You do this by demonstrating your willingness to live without the very thing your offender is threatened by. If it's a position on the job, you must show your offender your willingness to live without that position. If it's favor with a parent or family member, you must show that offender your willingness to live without that favor. In fact, you may even want to forgo the favor that's intended for you and instead give it to your offender as a blessing. When someone is threatened by your "metaphorical place" in line ahead of them, you must be secure enough to offer them your spot. Your willingness to live without the very thing they desire will have a greater impact on them than any act of retaliation ever could.

"Self Wants to Stay Alive"

The man who lives by the self-principle focuses on what must be done in order to stay alive. That doesn't mean that he hates or dislikes people. Nor does it mean that he fails to engage in acts of kindness or compassion towards others. What it does mean is that if it comes down to him dying or someone else dying, that man will first try to keep himself alive above all other things. This is "the way of the world." Even Satan believes this to be true. That's why Satan petitioned God for the right to damage Job's physical body. "Skin for skin!" Satan replied. "A man will give all he has for his own life. But stretch out your hand and strike his flesh and bones, and he will surely curse you to your face." (Job 2:5) Now that's scary when Satan feels like he's got mankind's self-centeredness so easily figured out. But Satan is absolutely convinced that when it all boils down, a man will always be more concerned about his own well-being than he will be about anyone or anything else. And as horrible as this statement sounds, is it true? If not, why don't we as individuals give more sacrificially to others? Why don't we give more sacrificially to God? What's holding us back? Why is it such a newsworthy event whenever someone sacrifices their life for another person? "The world" is actually SHOCKED whenever someone deviates from the self-principle. Whether it's an act of public service, charity, heroism, or sheer goodwill, people are always mystified whenever they lay witness to an act that's completely void of self-interest. Even when doing something as simple as holding the door for someone, or letting someone go ahead of us in line, acts of selflessness always seem to evoke some type of surprise or awe from others around us. To the human mind, it's really hard to conceive someone completely giving up their life for another individual. But to the human spirit, no action in the world is more attractive.

"Death Rules the Christian"

Just as the self-principle rules "the world," "the death-principle" rules the Christian. The death-principle is quite different from the self-principle described in the preceding paragraph. Unlike the self-principle, which is driven by "preservation of life," the death-principle is driven by "relinquishment of life." It would be contradictory for a Christian to try and keep themselves alive at the expense of someone else. In fact, the Christian is tasked with just the opposite. **The Christian's primary goal in life is to give their life to Christ and submit to the Holy Spirit in a way that creates a willingness to "die to self" so that others may live**. The biblical term for this is called "love."

The death-principle doesn't stipulate that the Christian can't give to self. Nor does it stipulate that the Christian can't partake in self-gratifying endeavors. What it does mean is that when it all boils down, the Christian is more concerned about relying upon the power of Christ to help others experience life, than he is about using his own strength to keep himself alive. **This complete and unfettered reliance upon the power of Christ is called "dying-to-self."** It's through this process that the Christian enters an abundant, Spirit-filled walk in Christ. It's through this process that the Christian enters a life of greatness. A life laid down unto Christ is true life.

"Self-Centeredness to Christ-Centeredness"

Jesus Christ came to earth in the express image of God. He lived a sinless life, was crucified for the sins of humanity, died, resurrected, ascended into heaven, and left mankind with this incredible gift called the Holy Spirit. When a man submits himself to this truth, professing Jesus Christ as Lord and Savior, receiving HIS spirit, and renewing his mind; he begins the lifelong process of transitioning from self-centeredness to Christ-Centeredness.

A man enters a state of righteousness the moment he accepts Christ into his heart and receives forgiveness for his sins. But it takes time for that man to transition from his old life of self-centeredness to his new life of Christ-Centeredness. It takes time for his mind to be renewed and delivered from a legacy of self-centered behavior.

Over the course of my marriage, I have exercised countless

demonstrations of self-determined, self-willed, self-centered behavior. And even though I've been in a relationship with Jesus Christ throughout my entire marriage, I've still struggled to purge the legacy of fear and self-centeredness that once dominated my life prior to Christ. And even as I write this book, I continue to confront these same challenges in making the transition from self-centeredness to Christ-centeredness.

"Death: The Ultimate Demonstration of Love"

When a husband lays down his life for his wife, he demonstrates love at its highest form. Jesus demonstrated love at its highest form by dying on a cross for mankind, even when mankind wanted nothing to do with Him. And likewise, the godly husband must show his love for his wife by dying for her in spite of her behavior towards him. The godly husband must work through his death-related fears in order to love his wife in the way that God calls him to. If a husband fears his own death, fights to stay alive, or puts a greater premium on his own life than he does his wife's life, he'll never walk at the level of freedom necessary to sacrifice his life for her. This is the godly husband's first step towards loving his wife. He must confront his own fear of death.

Chapter 2

A Husband's Walk With God

The Husband's Greatest Discovery

"Salvation is found in no one else, for there is no other name under heaven given to men by which we must be saved."

Acts 4:12

The Husband's Revelation of Jesus Christ

The husband discovers many things over the course of his life. He discovers his likes, his dislikes, his tolerance levels, his limitations, his stressors, his frustrations, his strengths, his weaknesses; all while discovering his purpose, how to be a husband, how to be a father, how to be a son, how to be a brother, how to be a friend, and most importantly, how to be a child of God. Without question there's a lot on the husband's plate. But there's no greater discovery in a husband's life than the discovery of who Jesus Christ is. Nothing is more critical to the future of a man or his family than this central discovery.

When a husband accepts Jesus Christ as his Lord and Savior, he does so because the true identity of Jesus has been revealed to his heart. It's not an action that he psychologically conjures up. Nor is it something that he tries to do as some type of good deed or gesture (all the good deeds in the world couldn't unlock the revelation of who Jesus Christ is). The revelation of Jesus Christ is a gift from God that was set aside for the husband from before earth was created.

Throughout the husband's life, the revelation of Jesus speaks softly, consistently, and assuredly to his heart. For years he tries to ignore the message, but he eventually comes to the place where he can no longer resist the truth that so profoundly speaks to his heart. This is the point in the husband's life where he finally comes to terms with the fact that Jesus Christ is the physical expression of the invisible God; and that he lived, died on a cross, and resurrected in order to save him. This officially marks the husband's acceptance of God's gift, and his transition from death to life. This is where the husband's journey of self-discovery begins; a journey that will inevitably lead him to the truth about himself.

The Husband's Lineage

A husband is heir to his mother and father through his natural lineage; but he is heir to Jesus Christ through his spiritual lineage. A husband is born first the natural way; but his second birth occurs when he is born of the Spirit of God. It's when he accepts the gift of salvation (through faith in Christ) that his spiritual rebirth begins. This is what it means for a husband to be "born again." Through the rebirth, the husband becomes "a new creation" in Christ, and dismantles the legacy of death that once plagued him.

It's the husband's faith in the promise of Christ that makes him "righteous" in God's sight. Abraham had faith in God's promise that he would one day father a great nation even though he had no children at the time; and because of his faith in God's promise, he was given righteous standing in God's sight. Similarly, when a husband demonstrates faith in the promise of God through Jesus Christ, he is also deemed righteous in God's sight. This gives the born-again husband and Abraham a special kinship; as both are connected through the same faith lineage. It's the husband's faith lineage that represents his true ancestry. It's his faith lineage that validates his identity in Christ. No other influence (whether cultural, social, political, economic or religious) will ever supersede the influence that comes by virtue of the husband's faith lineage.

The Husband's Deliverance Part 1 – "Salvation"

Even after the husband's rebirth and the establishment of

his faith lineage, he will continue to encounter many things that offer him a path to deliverance. Money, sexual gratification, power, and status are just a few of the things that guise as cure-all's for each and every one of the husband's perceived needs.

It may sound crazy, but some born again men actually seek deliverance in people. In fact, it's not uncommon for a godly man to place his friends, family, loved ones, or even his supervisor in the position of savior. Some men are actually stuck at a difficult place in their life because they're still waiting for that loved one to grant them the salvation that they desire. They're still waiting for salvation from that father who failed to accept them growing up. They're still waiting for salvation from that family member who abused them as a child. They're still waiting for salvation from that spouse who cheated on them. Men look for salvation in things and people that are clearly incapable of saving them. There's only one who is capable of shouldering the awesome burden of savior. It is through Him (and Him alone) that a man finds deliverance. If ever a man tries to find deliverance in any other place, he will most certainly find himself empty.

The Husband's Deliverance Part 2 – "Lordship"

Salvation in Christ is just the first step towards the husband's deliverance; the next step is Lordship. The husband's salvation in Christ takes place instantaneously, but his deliverance takes place over time, as he progressively makes Jesus Christ Lord over his life. Lordship involves making every aspect of the husband's life subject to the will of Christ, including his identity, his hopes, his dreams, his time, his finances, his thoughts, his desires, his actions, his emotions, and his relationships. When a husband entrusts these things to Christ, it's only a matter of time before he conforms to the image of the one who created him.

The Husband's Deliverance Part 3 – "Mind Renewal"

The third and final step in the husband's journey towards deliverance is mind renewal. Mind renewal goes hand in hand with Lordship (step 2 of deliverance). The mind is the epicenter of the husband's world, and is intricately tied to the desires of his heart. It will be hard, if not impossible for the husband to make Jesus Christ Lord over his affairs without first gutting out his old way of thinking.

A husband is transformed into the image of Christ to the degree that he renews his mind (Romans 12:2). And the fruit of his salvation will be evident to the degree that he possesses the Mind of Christ. Without a change in the husband's thinking, deliverance will perpetually elude him. Below are five steps that will help the husband navigate the very intricate process of mind renewal:

Step #1: "Admit the Need for Mind Renewal"

To start the process of mind renewal, the husband must first confront the fact that his mind (as it exists today) operates in a fatally flawed state. He must accept the fact that his present mind needs renewal in order for him to experience the complete deliverance that God is trying to offer him. For many husbands, that's a very difficult thing to do. It's difficult for a man to accept the fact that there are parts of his mind that need renewal. It's difficult for a man to accept the fact that his thought process has to change. It's difficult for a man to come face-to-face with himself. A man must take the courage to openly confess his need for mind renewal. If he cannot do this, it will cause a major impediment to his deliverance in Christ.

Step #2: "Know Your Influences"

After the husband admits his need for mind renewal, he must then confront those things that have contributed to the shaping and fashioning of his mindset. Every past and present influence within the husband's life must be examined, including his family, his upbringing, his culture, his friends, his religion, his education, and any other thing that's played a pivotal role in his overall development. **When a husband identifies those people and experiences that collectively contribute to his worldview, he also identifies those people and experiences that pose the greatest threat to his mind renewal.**

Step #3: "Know Your Path"

Though the source of each man's deliverance is the same (Jesus Christ), the path of each man's deliverance is as complex and diverse as the stars in the sky. *Simply put, each man's path to deliverance is different.* Therefore, each man must understand his own unique path. The man who was exposed to pornography as a child will experience a different mind renewal path than the man who encountered physical abuse. The man who grew up without a father will experience a different mind renewal path than the man with a history of substance abuse. The man who was raised by a single mother will experience a different mind renewal path than the man who was abandoned by both of his parents. And even in those situations where a husband shares similar life experiences with another man, the manner by which he renews his mind is still unique unto him. No man's path to deliverance is the same. A husband must take the time to understand and explore those unique, deeply rooted issues that have plagued him over the course of his life. Whether it's sexual addiction, low self-esteem, drug abuse, anger issues, or self-centered behavior, a man must understand the unique path of mind renewal required for his deliverance.

Step #4: "Submit to Something Greater"

A husband initiates the process of mind renewal by "opening himself to receive." This means that the husband must open his heart to something in order for his mind to follow. Attempting to renew a man's mind without first soliciting his heart's cooperation is like trying to fly a kite without wind. We understand that simply thrusting a kite into the air won't make it fly. And likewise, the mere thrusting of information into a man's mind will not in itself translate into mind renewal. There must be something greater to ignite this process.

If a man says to himself, "I am the greatest" one hundred times, that doesn't necessarily mean that his mind will be renewed with greatness. If man only listens to the most positive messages of hope and inspiration, that doesn't necessarily mean that his mind will be renewed with hope and inspiration. Renewal of the mind doesn't come automatically by way of positive speaking, listening, or seeing. These things are all extremely helpful, but cannot alone ignite the mind renewal process. Mind renewal is first and foremost ignited through submission. **Submission by definition is the voluntary or involuntary acceptance of influence.** So when a man submits himself to something, he subjects himself to that particular thing's influence. This is where the process of mind renewal begins.

A husband must submit himself to "something" in order to ignite the mind renewal process. But he can't just submit himself to "anything." He must submit to something greater than himself. If a husband merely submits to his own knowledge and power, he relegates himself to his own knowledge and power. This makes the husband's mind limited by default, and renders him incapable of expanding his potential in God. If a husband wants to renew his mind, his heart must be submitted to something greater than himself.

Step #5: "Distinguish Your Spirit, The Holy Spirit and The Sinful Nature"

There are three active agents at work inside the godly husband at all times: (1) The Human Spirit, (2) The Holy Spirit, and (3) The Sinful Nature. Nothing influences the mind of a godly husband more than these three things; nor does anything more profoundly impact his life. If a man wants to renew his mind, he must understand these three influences, and how each relates to the totality of his development.

"The Human Spirit"

The human spirit is the essence of man's being. It is an amalgamation of his innermost beliefs, desires, motivations, and appetites. The human spirit is also a container. Therefore a man must always be aware of the things that attempt to occupy it. The biggest threat to the husband's spirit container is any other spirit that attempts to occupy it apart from the Spirit of God. The bible makes mention of many different types of spirits that exist in the world. It references evil spirits, unclean spirits, impure spirits, deceiving spirits, haughty spirits, spirits of dizziness, spirits of despair and spirits of prostitution. All of these spirits seek to occupy man's spiritual container, with the ultimate goal of destroying the husband. A husband must be aware of this, or he'll unknowingly invite spirit-led things and people into his life that wish to bring him harm.

"The Holy Spirit"

The Holy Spirit reveals the life and personality of God inside of the husband. He is the most prolific and accurate voice within the husband's life. He speaks to husband each and every day, giving him guidance and insight according to the knowledge of God's will. Just as the human spirit reflects the essence of man's being, so does the Holy Spirit reflect the essence of God's being. The bible describes the Holy Spirit as one that: (1) encourages, (2) baptizes (spiritually), (3) permits, (4) restricts, and (5) warns concerning things to come. No other voice is more important than the voice of the Holy Spirit; for He alone understands how the husband's choices tie into his ultimate destiny.

"The Sinful Nature"

The Sinful Nature is the sin proclivity etched into man's body as a result of Adam's original transgression. It is the sin DNA passed down over the course of human history. The bible commonly refers to this as "the flesh." A newborn child doesn't need training on how to be selfish. That child will think and act selfishly from the moment he is born, because the sin proclivity for selfishness is already etched inside of him. It's only as a man grows that he learns how to selflessly focus on the needs of others around him.

All men have that remnant of sin inside their physical bodies, even those who profess salvation in Christ. In fact, no matter how much a man gives himself to the Lord, no matter how much he studies, prays, worships, and fasts unto God, he still must battle the sinful proclivities that reside inside of him. This is a battle that a man will endure for the rest of his life. It's only after Jesus returns to the earth that a man's body will be raised "imperishable," free from any sin, sickness, disease, deterioration, or death.

"The Holy Spirit Versus The Sinful Nature"

The Holy Spirit and the Sinful Nature both produce fruit within the husband's body. The Holy Spirit produces the fruit of "love, joy, peace, forbearance, kindness, goodness, faithfulness, gentleness and self-control." (Galatians 5:22-26) The Sinful Nature produces the fruit of "sexual immorality, impurity and debauchery; idolatry and witchcraft; hatred, discord, jealousy, fits of rage, selfish ambition, dissensions, factions and envy; drunkenness, orgies, and the like..." (Galatians 5:19-20)   The fact that these two diametrically opposed fruits actually originate from the same body is absolutely amazing. But what's even more amazing is the fact that these two fruits operate inside of the husband, side by side as wheat and tare, even as the husband grows. This provides context for the (sometimes) contradicting behaviors of godly husbands. It explains why a husband can sometimes find himself doing the very thing that he hates, and other times ignoring the very thing that he loves. It's because the husband struggles to reconcile these two opposing fruits working inside of him at the same time. This is the husband's greatest source of conflict, and can only be overcome as he "lives according to the Holy Spirit." (Galatians 5:16)

Step #6: "Live According to The Holy Spirit"

Each day, the godly husband is confronted with many difficult decisions. But by far the most difficult decision that he has to make is where he will derive his daily power source. His power source will come from only one of two places; the Holy Spirit or the Sinful Nature. Both power sources will beckon him over the course of any given day, but only one he will answer. One day he may answer the call of discord, another day he may answer the call of peace. One day he may answer the call of rage, another day he may answer the call of self-control. Each day the husband makes the critical choice of which voice he will answer. And the choice that he makes will ultimately become his destiny.

Which Power Source Will You Submit To?

It doesn't really matter which power source calls the

husband. Both the sinful nature and Holy Spirit will repeatedly call upon the husband over the course of any given day. The only thing that matters is which power source the husband submits to. Whichever power source the husband submits to ultimately determines how his mind is renewed. If the husband submits to the call of the Holy Spirit, and lives according to its dictates, his mind will be renewed in a way that reflects the desires of The Holy Spirit. If the husband submits to the call of the sinful nature, and lives his life according to its dictates, his mind will be renewed in a way that reflects the desires of the sinful nature. Ultimately, whatever power source the husband submits himself to fuels how he lives, and how he lives fuels his mindset. And with every subsequent act of submission, the husband's lifestyle and mindset becomes more and more settled.

Submitting to the Holy Spirit – "The Practical Application"

Let's examine this on a practical level. Imagine that on a particular day, the Holy Spirit prompts a man's to apologize after an argument that he has with his wife. He's comfortable with the idea, so he decides to apologize. However, after a few moments of deliberation, his flesh (the Sinful Nature) tells him that his apology may not be such a good idea, and that it will most likely hinder, rather than help his wife in abandoning her selfish ways.

Now at this point, the husband has two different voices soliciting him; the voice of "apology" and the voice of "no apology." After taking a few minutes to assess both voices, he makes the decision not to apologize. But as the evening progresses, thoughts of apologizing once again begin beckoning him. This time, the prodding of the Holy Spirit is much stronger than it was before. Now the man feels a deep sense of conviction that he hadn't felt previously. This causes him to strongly rethink his decision. After a few moments of back and forth in his mind, he decides to reverse his decision and apologize to his wife. Later that evening, he apologizes just as the Spirit prompted him to.

The man in the above example was given a "call to action" from both The Holy Spirit and the Sinful Nature. The man battled back and forth as to which invitation he would accept, but in the end he accepted the Holy Spirit's invitation. When he took that final step and apologized, he essentially "followed" or "lived" according to the Holy Spirit. He submitted himself to the Spirit of God, and his choice to apologize followed.

By making the decision to apologize to his wife, a power

was released into this man's life that enabled him to accomplish what the spirit desired. It's a power that could not be transferred until this man crossed the threshold of obedience. If this man had instead disobeyed and opted to follow the sinful nature's invitation; his mind would have then become aligned with those things that the sinful nature desired. Not only would he have rejected the Spirit's invitation to apologize, but any future invitations to apologize from the Spirit would have likely been ignored or dismissed.

"Submission Leads to Lifestyle - Lifestyle Leads to Mindset"

➤ "Those who live according to the Spirit have their minds set on what the spirit desires." (Romans 8:5)

➤ "Roll your works upon the Lord [commit and trust them wholly to Him; He will cause your thoughts to become agreeable to His will, and] so shall your plans be established and succeed." (Proverbs 16:3 - AMP)

These scriptures reveal to us just how much our living shapes our mindset. Essentially, the more we give ourselves to certain life choices, the more embedded those life choices become in our way of thinking. But even as scripture reveals just how much our living shapes our mindset, the scripture also reveals just how much our "mindset shapes our living." Romans 10:9 says that "a man will be transformed by the renewal of his mind." Proverbs 23:7 (KJV) says that "as a man thinketh in his heart, so is he." There's no question that a man's mindset impacts his living, even as his living impacts his mindset. But the entire process begins with submission. It's submission that ultimately fashions how a man lives; which fashions his mindset, which fashions his submission. Each affects the other in succession; with submission being the ultimate catalyst for the entire process.

"Mind Renewal: Conclusion"

The godly husband's mind renewal encompasses five critical elements: (1) admission that his mind needs renewal, (2) knowing his influences, (3) knowing his path, (4) preparing himself to submit to something greater (5) recognizing the distinction between his spirit, The Holy Spirit and his Sinful Nature, and (6) living according to the Holy Spirit. All six of these things collectively contribute to the husband's transformation. However, the tipping point in the husband's mind renewal process occurs at the point of submission.

Even when a godly husband submits to something as simple as an urge, (whether good or bad) choices that support those urges are certain to follow. If, for example a husband repeatedly submits to an urge for food, his mind will eventually become governed by a desire for food. If a husband repeatedly submits to an urge for sex, his mind will eventually become governed by a desire for sex. **Each time that man submits to an urge, whether it be an urge for food or an urge for sex, it becomes harder and harder for him to reject that urge when it comes around again. A husband's mind will always be fixated on those things that he repeatedly gives himself to.**

When a husband gives himself to the Holy Spirit, his mind will be renewed in accordance with the desires of the Holy Spirit. Through submission, the husband is empowered to live out his Sprit-led choices, and walk with a greater sensitivity towards the things of the Spirit.

Chapter 3

A Husband's Personal Responsibility

The Husband Must Take Full Responsibility

"Look, she is your servant, do as you see fit."

Genesis 16:5

"The First Law of Responsibility"

The first and most important law of responsibility is that responsibility cannot be leased, chartered or rented; responsibility must be owned. Without ownership, responsibility is nothing more than an optional, non-binding suggestion. However, with ownership, responsibility transcends from a mere invitation into a duty. And it's the "duty" that establishes the mandate to action. This is the core essence of responsibility. A godly husband must understand this fundamental law of ownership before he tries to understand anything else about the subject. A husband will continuously struggle with responsibility until he makes the transition from "renting" to "owning" his world.

"Groomed for Ownership"

From the very first day that a little boy receives his first toy, he is being tested for the aptitude to own. If he takes good care of one toy, he makes himself eligible for yet another toy. If he takes care of his two toys, he makes himself eligible for yet a third toy, and a fourth toy, and so the pattern continues. If at any point the young boy fails in his ability to show good stewardship over his toys, he puts himself at risk of having limitations set on how many toys he can possess.

The young boy then moves to elementary school where he's given books, pencils, rulers, and homework, and is measured according to how well he manages these things. From there he moves on to middle school and high school where he's given ownership over more homework, grades, extra-curricular activities and relationships. From there the young man goes to college, where he's given ownership over more of the same, including relationships with professors, roommates, friends, and university administrators. He stays in a dormitory or an apartment and owns responsibility for the care and maintenance of that as well. From college, the young man enters the workforce and takes ownership over his career, his professional development, his finances, his living arrangements and more profound levels of relationship involvement.

"The Ultimate Ownership Test"

The young man reaches the apex of his ownership

44

experience when he confronts "the ultimate ownership test." The ultimate ownership test gauges the young man's sense of maturity and willingness to shoulder responsibility over a long period of time. This test tells the world in no uncertain terms "he's ready." The ultimate ownership test is simply this: Is this young man willing and able to: (1) Confront his true self (2) Take ownership of his thoughts, actions and behaviors (past, present and future) (3) Commit to a lifelong relationship with a woman (4) Take ownership of that woman's life (past, present, and future) and (5) Love that woman unconditionally. If the young man is willing and able to do these five things, he passes the ultimate ownership test; also known as, "the marriage test."

Up until that point in the young man's life, all of his ownership experiences dealt with things and people within his span of control (i.e. his toys, his school supplies, his grades, his friendships). But the marriage test is different. The marriage test deals with things and people outside the young man's span of control. The marriage test focuses on how external things behave and whether or not the young man is willing to take ownership for those things. **The marriage test challenges a man to accept a lifetime ownership for something he has no control over, without a clue of what that thing might look like in fifty years.** It's no longer about a man owning "his toys." It's about a man owning his toys, while at the same time owning his wife's toys that he has no control over. And he must do this in a way that facilitates oneness with her over the course of a lifetime. Now that's serious business!

"Marriage Must Be Fully Owned"

When a man makes a commitment to marry, it's not a partial or conditional stake venture. He can't lease it, rent it, timeshare it, or sub-contract it out. It's something that he owns outright and complete, right down to the results and/or consequences that arise from it. He owns this commitment outright, not because the laws of his state says he does, but because God Himself says he does.

A husband doesn't commit to oneness in his marriage "if and only if" his wife cooperates. He commits to oneness in his marriage regardless of whether his wife cooperates, because God gave him the responsibility to become one with his wife, and that's all that matters. Similarly, a husband takes full responsibility for his marriage regardless of whether or not his wife takes full responsibility because God has given him the mandate to take full responsibility for his marriage.

Some husbands may ask the question, "Isn't my wife fully responsible to God for our marriage as well?" To this I would say, "Absolutely," your wife is fully responsible unto God for your marriage just as you are. But that's an issue between her and God. And likewise, God should be the one to contest if ever there's a problem with her fulfilling those responsibilities.

"Partial vs. Full Responsibility"

There's a big difference between a husband who takes "partial responsibility" and one who takes "full responsibility." The husband who takes full responsibility is willing to take ownership for "all things" concerning his marriage. Conversely, the husband who takes partial responsibility is only willing to own "some things" concerning his marriage. The difference between a husband who takes full responsibility one who takes partial responsibility is the difference between a mature husband and an immature husband. The more things that a husband is willing to own within his marriage, the more mature he proves himself to be. The fewer things that a husband is willing to own within his marriage, the less mature he proves himself to be. The correlation between a man's willingness to own and his level of maturity is irrefutable.

"The Three Essential Traits of Responsibility"

The acceptance of responsibility requires three essential traits. If a husband fails to consistently practice these three traits, he will undoubtedly fail in his acceptance of responsibility. I've assembled some insights below to help explain how each of these traits plays a role in the acceptance of full responsibility. Study these insights carefully and think about how they relate to your overall growth and development as a husband.

Element #1: "Accountability"

The first trait of responsibility is "accountability." The husband who makes himself accountable owns the task of answering for whatever it is he's accountable for. Whenever a problem arises (whether through his own wrongdoing or through someone else's wrongdoing) that man must be willing to stand up and answer for it. If a man's wife does something wrong, that man must be willing to stand up and answer on his wife's behalf. If a man's child makes a poor decision, that man must be willing to stand up and answer on that child's behalf. Accountability in a nutshell is "answerability."

A man's "answering for his wife" doesn't mean that he usurps his wife's voice. Nor does it mean that he has a license to clarion call his wife's shortcomings to the world. Accountability is not about a husband telling the world all the wrong his wife has committed. Accountability simply means that a husband is willing to stand in his wife's place and answer for any and all charges against her (even if those charges come from him). It means that he's her advocate, and as such, he must represent her to the fullest, despite her wrongdoing. This is what makes a man accountable. This is the first step towards acceptance of full responsibility.

Element #2: "Culpability"

The next element of responsibility is "culpability." Culpability by definition is a husband's willingness to accept fault. This takes the husband beyond a mere willingness to answer for his wife. Whereas answerability says "I'm willing to answer for my wife," culpability says, "not only am I willing to answer for my wife, I'm also willing to accept fault for her as well." A husband becomes culpable when he says, "I'm wrong," "I did it," "It's my fault," "It's my mistake."

In the book of Genesis chapter 16, Sarah challenged her husband Abraham to accept culpability for what transpired between him and her maidservant, Hagar. Just a few months earlier, Sarah recommended that Hagar have sexual relations with Abraham so that she could bear a child on her behalf. Abraham followed Sarah's recommendation and proceeded to impregnate Hagar. But after Hagar conceived, Sarah began reconsidering her decision. As the pregnancy progressed, Sarah started to regret her decision. By the time Ishmael was born, Sarah altogether despised her decision and everything associated with it (especially Hagar). To Sarah, Hagar was nothing more than a vivid reminder of an extremely poor decision. So with great pain in her heart, Sarah re-directed her frustration towards her husband. "It's all your fault!" Sarah said to Abraham. "I put my servant into your arms, but now that she's pregnant she treats me with contempt. The LORD will show who's wrong—you or me!" (Gen 16:5 NLT)

Sarah was challenging Abraham to accept culpability for her pain. This isn't unusual in a marriage, as often times a husband will be asked to bare culpability, even when his wife is also at fault. This isn't an easy pill for the husband to swallow. And in this case, rather than swallowing the pill of culpability, Abraham instead says to Sarah, **"Look, she is your servant, so deal with her as you see fit."** Abraham shifts the burden of culpability back onto Sarah, and detaches himself from her present condition. He also rejects culpability for all that's transpired through his decision to lay with Hagar. When a husband rejects culpability, he rejects responsibility.

Element #3: Liability

Probably the most difficult part of accepting responsibility is owning the blame and the consequences that come about as a result of our choices. When a husband accepts both the blame and the consequences that come about as a result of his choices, he assumes "liability." Liability is the "paying the price" arm of responsibility. It's when a husband says to his wife, "I will pay the price for your transgressions, no matter how much they cost, even if they are committed against me."

What husband is willing to pay the price for his wife's sin? There are certainly many husbands who would be willing to answer for their wife's sins, and even some would be willing to accept fault for their wife's sins. But it's a completely different ballgame when a husband is asked to "pay the price" for his wife's sins. Some husbands have enough difficulty taking the blame for their own sins, not to mention the sins of their wives. If anything, a husband might be inclined to offload the weight of his sin in order to ease the burden of his guilt. This is what sin bearers do. They try and pass the burden of sin along to others to avoid their own demise. That's why it was easy for Adam to tell God, "The woman you gave me…" That's why it was easy for Abraham to tell Sarah, "Look, she (Hagar) is your servant, do as you see fit." That's why it was easy for the man at the pool of Shalom to say "I have no one to help me…" instead of answering Jesus' question about whether or not he wanted to be healed (John 5:6). The acceptance of blame represents death to a man. And as I stated earlier, no man wants to die, every man wants to live. This is why blame is so prevalent within today's society.

"Jesus Makes Himself Liable"

Jesus assumed the ultimate liability by sacrificing himself and shouldering the blame for the sins of the world. But this wasn't just any sacrifice, it was a sacrifice that Christ made for his bride (the church) who needed his death in order for her to experience freedom. This is the model that Jesus established for husbands. **If a man wants to follow in this model, he must live his life as a propitiating sacrifice, willing and able to pay the price for sins belonging not only to himself, but his wife, and any other thing that God entrusts to his care.**

"Liability of Lateness"

What does a husband's propitiating sacrifice look like? To help make the image a bit more tangible, let's explore an area that tends to be a challenge between husbands and wives, "lateness." Let's say that a man's wife is running late for an event that they're scheduled to attend as a couple. The chances are high that the man will be upset with his wife at the point that they're finally ready to leave the house. Not only that, but it's also likely that he'll continue to be upset with her as they drive to the event. Now when the couple finally arrives at their intended destination, the husband will most likely do one of three things: He will either: (1) walk in and repress all of his frustration and embarrassment, (2) transfer the weight of his frustration and embarrassment onto his wife by publically proclaiming that "she made them late," or (3) he will accept blame for his wife's failings and own their lateness "as a couple." If the husband is visiting a familiar place, there's a good chance he'll choose option 2, and let everyone know that "his wife was the reason they were late."

The husband who assumes liability does not publically exploit his wife's deficiencies, nor does he distance himself from her sin. As a propitiating sacrifice, the husband is willing to shoulder the burden of her lateness upon himself. In other words, "she" wasn't late, "we" were late.

Please understand, this does not mean that the husband in any way contributed to his wife's lateness (although he very well could have by not supporting and encouraging his wife as she got ready to leave). Nor does it mean that the husband failed to get ready in a timely manner. What it does mean is that the family "as an entity" failed to hit the desired mark, and as a result, the husband takes the blame for that shortfall. The bible refers to this sacrificial relationship between husband and wife as "covering." When a husband covers for his wife, he tells the world, "I'll take the blame for her regardless of my involvement," "I'll pay the price," "I'll accept the consequences," "I'll burden the charges." **The husband ascends to the highest levels of responsibility when he becomes habitual about taking the blame for his own sins and the sins of his wife.** By taking the blame intended for his wife upon himself, the husband models one of God's greatest attributes. In doing so, he takes his last and final step towards the acceptance of responsibility.

"Accountability, Culpability and Liability Work Together"

Accountability, culpability and liability must all come together in order for full responsibility to take effect. If a husband tries to exercise one without the other, he'll repeatedly come up short in his quest to achieve this goal. A husband might be willing to answer for his wife's wrongdoings, but that doesn't necessarily mean he'll be willing to assume fault for her. And conversely, just because a husband is willing to accept fault for his wife, doesn't necessarily mean that he'll be willing to accept her blame. And if by chance the husband is willing to accept blame for his wife's wrongdoing, that doesn't necessarily mean that he won't argue the fact that it wasn't his fault.

"Patterns of Responsibility-Avoidance"

There are two dominant patterns of "responsibility avoidance" that husbands tend to get themselves trapped in.

I've assigned two commonly used legal terms to each pattern in order to help give them practical meaning. Review both patterns, and examine your life to see if there are any congruencies. Identifying your own personal patterns for accepting fault and blame are absolutely critical to understanding your propensity for accepting responsibility.

"Pattern #1: The No Contest Plea"

In the world of criminal law, defendants are given the opportunity to plead "Nolo Contendere," which in Latin literally means, "I do not wish to contend." In modern times, we call this the "no contest plea." the no contest plea carries with it all the penalties and consequences associated with a guilty plea, without a formal admission of the facts that support the allegations. It's the defendant's way of saying, "I'll accept the blame for what's transpired, but I don't agree with your version of the story." Or to put it in ITMOAGH terminology, "I'm liable but not culpable."

In the world of marriage, it's not unusual for a husband assume liability without culpability. In other words, it's not unusual for him to take the blame for something that his wife accuses him of; while at the same time feel as if he's done nothing wrong. When a husband does this, he accepts liability, without culpability. He accepts blame, but rejects wrongdoing. In a nutshell, he pleads "no contest" to his wife's charges against him. The no contest Plea causes strain within a marriage because it detaches the husband from his wife's claims against him. Below are a few examples of what "The No contest plea" looks like in a marriage relationship. Please know that this is a very dangerous plea pattern for the husband to adopt.

Example #1- A wife charges her husband with being overly-friendly/conversational with a female waitress while at a restaurant. The husband pleads guilty to the charge of having "a friendly" conversation with the waitress, but feels that his wife wrongly portrayed certain aspects of the conversation. The husband takes a "no contest" plea.

Example #2- A husband accidently offends his wife as he tries to encourage her to lose weight. The husband pleads guilty to his offense, but denies the manner in which the offense occurred. The husband takes a "no contest" plea.

Example #3- A husband is 30 days late in paying a particular bill, and his wife complains that he's "always" 60 or 90 days late. The husband accepts the blame for his lateness, but disputes the actual frequency of his lateness. The husband once again pleads "no contest."

In each of the above examples, the husband accepts blame, but won't agree to the specific facts involving his wrongdoing. This is the essence of the no contest plea.

Now, you may be thinking, "What if my wife's accusations against me are false? If that's the case, isn't the "no contest plea" correct?" Not necessarily. If a man's wife falsely alleges him of something, I would first encourage that man to think about Jesus, who was innocent of all` charges against him, but nevertheless took responsibility for those charges. He didn't argue with his accusers about their claims. He simply stated the truth, and accepted whatever false allegations that were made against him.

Likewise, a godly husband not need debate or argue with his wife concerning her claims against him. He only needs to state the truth as he knows it, and humbly accept whatever perception his wife has of him. It doesn't mean that his wife is right. It simply means that he's not going to fight his wife's perception of him. Because ultimately, it's never about the allegations that a wife makes against her husband, it's always about her perception of him. That's what drives her allegations. By pleading no contest, a man successfully defends himself against his wife's allegations, but does nothing to address her perception of him. **A man changes his wife's perception of him by assuming ownership of his wrongs, and by changing his ways.** This must be the husband's default focus at all times, rather than the no contest plea.

Pattern #2 - The Contributory Negligence Plea

The no contest plea lets a husband assume liability (blame) without admitting culpability (wrongdoing). The husband who makes such a plea tells himself, "I'll take the blame, even though I didn't do anything wrong." However, there's another type of plea in the world of civil law that lets a man assume culpability without admitting liability. This is called the "contributory negligence" plea. The contributory negligence plea lets a defendant enlist others in the blame for his wrongdoing. This plea essentially says to the world, "It's my fault, but I shouldn't have to pay for this on my own." Or to put it in ITMOAGH terminology, "I'm culpable, but not liable." Each and every day husbands find themselves pleading contributory negligence in response to their wives' charges against them.

Below are a few examples of what the contributory negligence plea looks like in a marriage relationship. Please note that like the no contest plea, the contributory negligence plea can also be a very dangerous one for the husband to adopt.

Example #1- A man raises his voice towards his wife after she tells him that he's "less than a man". The man claims contributory negligence, admitting his wrong for raising his voice, but feels his wife is partly to blame for provoking him.

Example #2- A man begins an affair with another woman after he's been emotionally neglected by his wife for an entire year. This man will claim contributory negligence, admitting his wrong for the affair, but blaming his wife for her being unavailable.

Example #3- A man refuses to speak to his wife because she embarrassed him at a recent family outing. This man will claim contributory negligence, admitting his wrong for not speaking to his wife, but blaming her for causing this situation.

Clearly the wife's behavior was not the best in each of the above examples; and God will hold the wife personally responsible for this. But this should never deter the husband's focus in accepting full responsibility. Responsibility is exclusive between God and the person He's given responsibility to. In all of these examples, both the husband and wife have their own individual responsibilities before God. A husband cannot lose sight of those responsibilities just because his wife abandons hers. If he does, he'll find himself in perpetual blame mode.

When Adam said to God, "The woman you gave me," after eating the forbidden fruit, he was essentially pleading contributory negligence; accepting fault for his role in the wrongdoing, but also distributing blame equally among Eve and God as well.

Final Thoughts on Taking Full Responsibility

There's enough blame and wrongdoing that occurs within a marriage to last a lifetime. How many times has a husband said, "Those are her bills, not mine!" "It's her fault that this happened, not mine!" "If she just treated me a little better this would have never happened!" Studies show that many wives end up divorcing their husbands simply because they refuse to accept responsibility for their actions. Most of these women would have been willing to work through their issues with their husbands if they saw a sincere willingness by them to address their wrongs and deal with the consequences of their actions. **When a man refuses to address his issues, his wife experiences a sense of futility that prevents her from seeing beyond her present condition.**

There are few things more critical to a man's development than his willingness to accept full responsibility. He cannot get in the habit of designating blame towards his wife whenever he does something wrong. He must ensure that the "no contest" and "contributory negligence" pleas are absent from his life.

Chapter 4

A Husband's Godly Responsibility

The Husband's Greatest Responsibility

"Jesus replied: 'Love the Lord your God with all your heart and with all your soul and with all your mind.' This is the first and greatest commandment."

(Matthew 22:37)

When a husband accepts Jesus Christ as his personal Lord and Savior, he assumes the greatest responsibility known to man. For starters, he takes ownership of the fact that there's sin in his life, and that this sin separates him from the God who created him. He also owns the fact that he cannot overcome this separation by his own strength, but instead must rely upon Jesus to reconcile the eternal gap between his sin and God's holiness. He embraces the word of God as his final authority and governor over his thinking and decision-making. And if he ever fails to live up to the tenants of his faith, he owns his failure completely. This is the level of responsibility that a man assumes when he gives his life to Jesus Christ. No other responsibility is greater than the one that a man has towards his creator.

The husband indeed assumes great responsibility when he accepts Christ into his life; but this in no way means that the scope of his responsibility ends there. The husband must now live out this new life that he's taken responsibility for. And the biggest part of this new life involves loving the Lord "with all his heart, soul and mind." (Matt 22:37)   Jesus refers to this as "God's greatest commandment."

The Husband's Second Greatest Responsibility

"And the second is like it: 'love your neighbor as yourself. All the law and the prophets hang on these two commandments.'"

(Matthew 22:37)

"Testing a Man's Love For God"

Any declaration of love must be accompanied by some sort of test to affirm the authenticity of profession. And so it is that a husband's love for God must be tested in order to establish its veracity. But how can we test whether a man loves God with all his heart, soul, mind and strength? Do we count how many times he attends church services during the week? Do we watch and see how frequently he prays? Do we send a survey to his friends and family asking them how committed he is to Christ during tough times? Even if we could quantify all of these things, it still would not provide a definitive test for whether or not a man loves God.

God reveals part of His definitive test for loving him in Matthew 22:39. This scripture is the technical equivalent of the preceding verse 37, but a much more tangible, pragmatic version. It simply reads, "Love your neighbor as yourself."

The statement "love your neighbor as yourself" completely revolutionizes the idea of what it means to love God. If I asked a thousand men what it means to love God, most all of them would say things like going to church, studying the bible, prayer, worship, and fasting. All of these things are great, but none of these things produce the biblical equivalent of loving God. Matthew 22:39 tells us that the biblical equivalent of loving God isn't prayer, fasting or going to church. The biblical equivalent of loving God is "loving your neighbor." No other command from God is more important than the command to love your neighbor. **As such, a man demonstrates his love for God through his love for people.**

A man can do a thousand things to show his love for God, but if he mistreats people in the process, he fails to love God. God is infinitely more concerned about a man's love for people, than he is about any other thing within a man's life. For the religious mind, this is a very hard thing to accept.

Love Test #1 – "Feeding The Sheep"

Jesus validates the test for loving God in John 21:15-17, where we see a series of exchanges that occur between Jesus and the apostle Peter. It begins with Jesus asking Peter the question, "Simon son of John, do you love me more than these?" To this Peter emphatically responds, "Yes, Lord, you know that I love you." Jesus then tells Peter, "Feed my lambs." Immediately afterwards, Jesus asks Peter another question, "Simon son of John, do you love me?" And again, Peter gives Jesus the same response, "Yes, Lord, you know that I love you." And to this Jesus says, "Take care of my sheep."

Now if ever there was a model for loving God, Jesus clearly defined it to Peter through this exchange. But that still wasn't enough for Jesus. He needed to ask Peter one last time, "Simon son of John, do you love me?" And this time Peter was hurt because Jesus had asked him three times if he loved him. So with disappointment in his heart, Peter gathered himself and humbly said to Jesus, "Lord, you know all things; you know that I love you." At this point, the test was finished, but Jesus wasn't done reinforcing the message. So again, Jesus reiterates to Peter, "Feed my sheep." With this, Jesus establishes the irrefutable blueprint for how to "love God." From that point forward, a man's love for God would no longer be measured by his religion; it would be measured by how well he cared for people.

Love Test #2 – "Caring For The Least of These"

In Matthew 25:40-45, Jesus takes the "loving God = loving people" test to a completely different level by establishing a direct correlation between God treatment and people treatment. Here Jesus not only conveys the importance of caring for those in need, but he actually goes one step further by personally taking on the identity of such individuals.

The scene begins with Jesus' depiction of the last days of judgment; a time when He returns as King to judge the world and separate the righteous from the unrighteous. Jesus begins his judgment with a blessing upon the righteous. He applauds them for their many kind acts towards him, among which include feeding Him when He was hungry, giving him drink when he was thirsty, and visiting Him when he was in prison.

As the righteous hear this, they are perplexed. "When did we see you hungry and feed you, or thirsty and give you something to drink?" they asked. To this Jesus responded, "Whatever you did unto the least of these, you did unto me." They didn't understand how the treatment of people and the treatment of God were correlated. But it didn't matter, because the righteous were committed to giving sacrificially regardless of whom the recipient was, or if there was a reward awaiting them in the end.

Jesus then moves on to the unrighteous. He begins their judgment by informing them that they are under a curse. He then explains that their curse came to fruition as a result of their neglect and unwillingness to take care of Him when he was in need. As the unrighteous hear this, they too are perplexed. "Lord, when did we see you hungry or thirsty or a stranger or needing clothes or sick or in prison, and did not help you?" they asked. To this Jesus replied, "Truly I tell you, whatever you did not do for one of the least of these, you did not do for me." The scriptural lesson here for the godly husband is that loving people isn't just a way to reflect God's love in us; loving people actually "is" loving God.

"Loving God Is Not Religious Activity"

Often times, a man will try and demonstrate his love for God by doing things unto Him. He lifts his hands unto God, he prays unto God, he cries unto God, he fasts unto God, he even gives his income unto God. He does everything in his power to show his love for God, but doesn't realize that these things in themselves do not "prove" love for God. The only thing that proves a man's love for God is how well he lives out the responsibilities contained in Matthew 22:39, John 21:15-17 and Matthew 25:40-45. In other words, how well does he live out the responsibility to "love people?"

A man can study the word of God, fast, pray, worship, and tithe, and still fail the Matthew 22:39 requirement to love his neighbor. A man can go to church every day of the week, attend every service, and even serve on the church staff, and yet still fail the John 21:15-17 mandate to care for God's sheep. A man's love for God is not validated by what he does for God. A man's love for God is validated by the love that he demonstrates towards people.

"Loving God - Conclusion"

Apart from believing in Jesus Christ, and embracing the finished work of the cross, there's no greater responsibility that a husband has, nor is there any greater test of his love for God, than his love for people. Through the husband's love for people, he demonstrates obedience to God, and proves that the love of God is in him.

If a man sees his wife in a prison, and chooses to walk away from her, he fails in demonstrating love towards God. When I say "prison," I'm not referring to those buildings made of concrete and steel. I'm referring to the prisons of fear, anxiety, insecurity, depression, and the like. If a husband sees his wife bound by these things and decides to abandon her, he fails in demonstrating love towards God. Even if the husband feels unequipped to deal with the weight of his wife's imprisonment, he still has the opportunity and responsibility to intercede for her through his prayers, his kindness, and his attentiveness.

I'm amazed whenever I think about the seriousness with which God takes our responsibility to love people. When God makes "loving people" the standard for eternal judgment; or when he fuses the identity of the unloved with his own identity; that tells me (in no uncertain terms) just how important "loving others" is to God. The godly husband must search his heart to determine whether or not he holds the same high value premium on love that his Heavenly Father does.

The Husband's Christian Responsibilities

"Therefore, as God's chosen people, holy and dearly loved, clothe yourselves with compassion, kindness, humility, gentleness and patience. Bear with each other and forgive one another if any of you has a grievance against someone. Forgive as the Lord forgave you. And over all these virtues put on love, which binds them all together in perfect unity."

Colossians 3:12-13

"The Love Test – Part II"

We began this chapter by looking at the one responsibility that trumps all other responsibilities in a husband's life, the responsibility to love God. Matthew 22:37 tells the husband to "love God with all your heart, soul, and mind." This is the husband's most significant responsibility. He must never lose sight of this. But as important as this responsibility is, it's equally important to know that this responsibility cannot be accomplished, except through Matthew 22:39, which says, "Love your neighbor as yourself." This creates an unmistakable congruency between loving God and loving people. This is the reason Jesus tells Peter in John 21, "If you love me, feed my sheep." This is the reason he tells the unrighteous in Matthew 25:40-45, "whatever you did not do for one of the least of these, you did not do for me." Jesus says these things because he knows that in order to love God effectively, you must love people effectively.

With such a great responsibility at hand, the godly husband must ask himself, "How do I live out my Christian responsibility to love people?" In the book of Colossians 3:12-14, Paul lays out eight virtuous responsibilities that collectively demonstrate the blueprint for loving people. I call these "the love responsibilities." As a husband lives out these eight responsibilities, he successfully demonstrates love for God.

Love-Responsibility #1: "Compassion"

The husband's first love-responsibility is compassion. **Compassion by definition is "a deep <u>identification with</u> and <u>sensitivity to</u> another person's hurt, pain, need or plight."** Compassion draws a man closer to the thing he has compassion for. A man cannot be detached from a particular thing and still have compassion for it. Compassion stirs a man in ways that cause him to roll up his sleeves and get intimately involved.

A great example of compassion is found in Luke 10:3, where a Samaritan extends assistance to a man who was beaten, robbed, and left for dead along the roadside. The Samaritan bandaged the wounds of the victim, gave him a place to stay, and took care of his debts until he got back on his feet. That is compassion. Compassion draws you close to people and their issues.

As a husband, one of the best things you can do for your wife is show compassion towards her. By drawing close to the issues that exist in your wife's life, you draw close to her heart. If she's hurt, you draw near to her hurt. If she's in pain, you draw near to her pain. Each day a husband gets a metaphoric opportunity to pick up his injured wife from along the side of the road, just as the Good Samaritan did. He has the opportunity to put bandages on her wounds, and provide her with a safe environment as she works through her healing process. He has the opportunity to cover her debts as his own, without counting them against her, or reminding her periodically about his goodwill. He has a responsibility to exercise compassion towards his wife each and every day.

Love-Responsibility #2: "Kindness"

The husband's second love responsibility is kindness. **Kindness by definition is warm-heartedness expressed through generosity and consideration towards others.** The operative word here is "warm-heartedness."

A man is kind because of the warmth that exists in his heart. It's the warmth in his heart that gives life to acts of generosity and consideration. If a man's heart is cold and callous, he'll act in cold and callous ways. A cold heart will never ask the question, "How can I support my wife?" Instead, the cold heart will ask, "Why does my wife deserve my support?"

A cold (or hardened) heart limits the husband's ability to exercise kindness towards his wife. Even if the husband mentally grasps the immense importance of kindness in his marriage, it will still be difficult for him to express it amidst the spiritual paralysis caused by a callous heart. A man makes the transition from cold-heartedness to warm-heartedness as he gives his callous heart to the Lord. As consumers, we understand how to take items back to the store if they're defective or incompatible for us. In the same way, we must learn how to return our calloused hearts to God in exchange for a new heart filled with joy and optimism. The husband must trust God to make the necessary heart exchange for him.

The bible says that the kindness of God leads a person to repentance (Romans 2:4). This means that kindness (at the very least) contains the power necessary to lead a person into a closer relationship with the Lord. Thus, the more kindness a man operates in, the better his chances are of leading his wife into a closer relationship with the Lord. The less kindness a man operates in, the lower his chances are of leading his wife into a closer relationship with the Lord. Kindness within a marriage is absolutely critical.

Love-Responsibility #3: "Humility"

The husband's third love responsibility is humility. **Humility by definition is "the volitional lowering of one's position, attitude, or status."** It occurs when a husband's heart has been sobered. Humility brings a husband low, so that he can adequately hear from others around him. Humility not only helps a man hear from others, it helps him listen as well; listen to body language, listen to eyes, listen to mannerisms, listen to hearts. A man needs all of these things in order to connect with others around him; especially his wife.

Whereas "humility" is the sobering of the human heart, "pride" is the elevation of the human heart. When a man's heart becomes elevated, it becomes increasingly difficult for him to exercise humility, because his heart disconnects from the rest of the world. In such a state, a man cannot see beyond his own perspective. A man must guard his heart against elevation so that he can remain open to the thoughts, feelings, and opinions of his wife. He must lower the premium that he has on his own position, attitude, and status. He must make the decision to humble himself.

Love-Responsibility #4: "Gentleness"

The husband's fourth love-responsibility is "gentleness." **Gentleness is "love applied softly."** This is the aspect of love that reveals meekness. I have found that there are essentially three types of people in the world: (1) Those who apply love toughly, (2) those who apply love gently, and (3) those who do not apply love at all. Many people like to apply love "toughly," This is called this "tough love." Tough love is when a person firmly and assertively tells another person the truth about themselves.

Husbands apply tough love towards their wives, kids, co-workers, and others that they come in contact with each and every day. Some husbands choose tough love to avoid being perceived as "soft" or "naive." Tough love can become a comfortable option for men, and in some instances does have its place. But love is most effective when its applied "softly." In 1 Corinthians 4:21 Paul asked the Corinthians, "What do you prefer? Shall I come to you with a rod of discipline, or shall I come in love and with a gentle spirit?" Paul gives the Corinthians one of two choices: "tough love" or "soft love." Paul encourages the Corinthians to embrace the latter. Why? Because soft love tends to convey a message of care and concern, while tough love on the other hand, is often perceived as uncaring and insensitive, despite the best of intentions.

A husband must "be gentle" with his wife. But not only must

he "be gentle" with her, he must also "appear gentle" through his demeanor and mannerism. In Matthew 11:29 Jesus says "Take my yoke upon you and learn from me, for I am gentle and humble in heart, and you will find rest for your souls." In Zechariah 9:9, the Lord prophetically tells Zechariah how He'll appear in both demeanor and stature upon his triumphant entrance into Jerusalem. He says to Zechariah, "Say to Daughter Zion, 'See, your king comes to you, gentle and riding on a donkey, and on a colt, the foal of a donkey.'" Through these scriptures, we learn that Jesus wasn't just gentle; He carried a gentle presence as well. A husband must always maintain a gentle presence before his wife and his children. They will look for this trait as he administers love "softly."

Love Responsibility #5: "Patience"

The husband's fifth love-responsibility is patience. **Patience by definition is calm endurance amidst difficult circumstance.** A man is not patient simply because he endures difficult circumstances; he is patient because while enduring difficult circumstances, he carries the essential trait of calmness. It's possible for a man to endure great trials, but at the same time impose great stress upon himself and everyone else around him. He may endure, but at the same time he's complaining, criticizing, and arguing all the way to the bitter end. This man would not be characterized as "patient" just because he endured a challenging time. He would need to exercise calmness. Where there is no calmness there is no patience.

Calmness is indeed the defining mark of patience. But what makes a man calm? To answer this we need to know where patience comes from. The scriptures tells us that that the fear of the Lord is the beginning of wisdom (Proverbs 19:11). That is where all wisdom begins; the fear of the Lord. But the scriptures also tell us that a man's wisdom yields patience (Proverbs 9:10). That means that patience is a direct result of the wisdom that exists within a man's life. The more wisdom a man has, the more patience that's produced inside of him.

So when we bring these two scriptures together, we see that patience is a bi-product of fearing the Lord. The greater a man's fear of the Lord is, the more godly wisdom he gains. The more godly wisdom he gains, the more relaxed and settled he becomes in trusting God. The more relaxed and settled he becomes in trusting God, the calmer he becomes. And the calmer a man is, the more patience he exercises.

People do all sorts of things to try and keep themselves calm; they drink coffee, they smoke, they drink alcohol, they engage all different types of mental and physical exercises just to de-stress the body. However, the most powerful way of de-stressing the body isn't through self medication. It's not even through the body's natural physiological provisions (i.e. through hormones such as oxcytocin, "the calming hormone"). The most powerful way to distress the human body is by walking in the fear of the Lord. Fear of the Lord distresses our body in ways that nothing else can. It's the fear of the Lord that infuses the wisdom that settles a man and puts his heart, mind and body at ease. This is what gives a man the confident trust in knowing that God is in control. It's confident trust in God that produces patience inside of a man. A husband must have the virtue of patience inside of him if he's going to effectively love his wife.

Love Responsibility #6: Bearing With Others

In life, we only occupy one of two dispositions. We either occupy a disposition of strength or we occupy a disposition of weakness. Thus, at any given point in time, within any given area, a man will either be strong or he will be weak. Romans 15:1 says that if a man finds himself in a position of strength, he should use that strength to "bear with the failings of the weak and not please himself." Conventional thought suggests that a man should use his own strength to please himself first. But that is not what the scripture commands. The scripture commands that the strength of the strong be used first to carry the weak. That whenever a husband finds himself in a position of strength, he should use that strength to help someone who is weaker than him.

Let's say for example, that a husband encounters someone who is rude or antagonistic towards him. It would be the husband's responsibility to use his strength to lovingly guide that person towards more acceptable behavior. Or let's say that a husband communicates well but his wife struggles in this particular area. That husband should lovingly use his strength to help his wife grow in her ability to communicate. When a husband uses his strength to bear the infirmities of those who are weak, he demonstrates his love for God.

A big part of the godly husband's love for his wife revolves around his ability to bear her weaknesses. In the beginning of a marriage, a husband's willingness to burden his wife's weaknesses is extremely strong. It's almost a delight for him to bear his wife's weaknesses at that early juncture of the relationship. But over the course of time, the weight of her weaknesses grows heavier upon him. Eventually, he gets to the place where he no longer wants to bear his wife's weaknesses at all. When the husband gets to this point in his marriage, he no longer represents that propitiating sacrifice modeled by Jesus Christ. A husband must not withhold strength from his wife when she needs it the most. Rather, he must use his strength to help inspire strength inside of his wife. A husband must be willing to identify his wife's weaknesses and bear them upon himself as if they were his own.

Love Responsibility #7: Forgiveness

"How many times should I forgive, seven times?" This question asked by Peter in Matthew 18:21 somehow suggests that forgiveness is some type of quantifiable, termed action measured by a recipient's just and earned deservedness. But Jesus turns that notion upside down in his response to Peter: "Not only seven times, but seventy-seven times." This is all it took for Jesus to show Peter the essence of forgiveness. Through these few words, Jesus taught Peter that forgiveness was not something to be measured. Nor was it something to be offered only when deemed deserved. Forgiveness is a way of life that runs as far as the stars in the sky and sands on the seashore. A man can no longer ask the question, "How much more do I have to put up with?" The number of times he forgives has no measure. In fact, it's probably unwise for him to keep count. John 3:34 says that God gives His Spirit to man "without limit." And likewise, a man extends forgiveness to his offenders in the same manner that God gives to him; "without limit."

Debt is the residual offspring of sin. So when a man retains sins (whether his sins or the sins of others) he retains debt unto himself. That makes unforgiveness a debt retention mechanism. As a man refuses to forgive the sins of his offenders, so he retains the sins of his offenders. This is different than "bearing the infirmities of someone who is weaker" (as discussed in the previous section). When a man bears someone else's weaknesses, he relies upon the power of Christ to carry that individual. But when a man practices unforgiveness, he relies upon his own power to carry the hurt, pain and struggle sown into his life by his perpetrators. In one situation, Christ carries the burden of sin, in the other situation; the non-forgiving man carries this burden.

Through unforgiveness, the husband becomes a debt container. Thus, whenever he holds a grudge, he carries debt. Whenever he languishes in resentment, he carries debt. Whenever he harbors thoughts of revenge, he carries debt.

Anytime he refuses to discharge the sins of his offender he assigns an immovable deficit unto himself. On the other hand, when a husband forgives, he reduces the debt in his life. So when he forgives the sins of his perpetrators, his burdens become lighter. This translates into a lighter walk for the husband.

There's no one better at discharging debt than the Lord Jesus Christ. Though treated unjustly and accused unfairly, He did not seek justice against his offenders; but rather, He sought mercy towards them. 1 Peter 2:23 says, "when He was reviled, did not revile in return; when He suffered, He did not threaten, but committed Himself to Him who judges righteously." The interesting thing here is that Jesus commits himself unto judgment rather than committing his adversaries unto judgment. He tells the Father, "examine me, not my adversaries." A husband must learn how to live his life in a similar fashion. As a daily practice, he must learn how to bring his own life under question before bringing his adversary's life under question. He must learn how to judge himself before he judges his adversaries. By doing so, the husband shows complete confidence that "the Father judges rightly." This keeps debt out of the husband's life and lays the groundwork for his willingness to forgive.

"Father forgive them" must be the anthem of every husband who wants to live out his love walk before the Lord. A husband must be strong enough to discharge the debt that's transferred to him by his offenders. And he doesn't have to worry about doing his offender a favor by forgiving them; because forgiveness is not about the offender. Forgiveness is about the person who's offended and their relationship with God. No offense is worth the husband jeopardizing his relationship with God. Forgiveness is not an option for the husband; it's one of the most important of all Christian responsibilities.

Conclusion: "A Husband's Christian Responsibilities"

We began this segment by examining the greatest of all Christian responsibilities, "love" and how it's expressed through the virtuous responsibilities set forth in Colossians 3:12-13 (compassion, kindness, humility, gentleness, patience, bearing with one another, and forgiveness). We said that all of these virtues represent different aspects of love that work together seamlessly in order to create perfect unity. In fact, Colossians states that love "binds" all of these virtues together.

The virtue of compassion works best when bound by love. The virtue of kindness works most best when bound by love. The virtue of humility works best when bound by love. Love is the sacrificial ingredient that brings life to all of these virtues.

If a husband tries to be compassionate without possessing the sacrificial ingredient of love, he'll show concern for his wife but will not want to get his hands dirty in the process. When a man doesn't want to get his hands dirty (i.e. by experiencing what his wife is experiencing, or feeling what she's feeling, or hurting as she's hurting) he will undoubtedly fail in his attempt to show compassion towards her. Trying to be compassionate without love is like trying to hug someone from 30 feet away. The man who seeks to love must draw neigh to the one he seeks to love. In the same way a man must draw neigh to the one that he seeks to show compassion for. A man must bring himself close to that person so that he can feel what they feel, hurt as they hurt, and see what they see. Without love, there's no sacrificial element within compassion that moves a man to say, "Even if I get dirty in the process of helping someone heal, that's ok." Or, "I'm willing to get myself dirty if that will help lead this person to a better place."

Think about humility without the sacrificial element of love. Without love, a person can appear humble in words and tone, yet walk with a very judgmental disposition towards others. The bible says that a man can warmly invite someone to partake of his food, but in his heart be against it. "Eat and drink he says to you, but his heart is not with you." (Proverbs 23:7 - KJV). On the surface the man appears to willing to share his food, but deep down he truly despises the idea. This is what happens when a man tries to project humility without possessing love. Love produces a sacrificial element within a man's life that moves him to examine himself and his shortfalls first before he examines anyone or anything else around him. It's love that helps a man enter an authentic place of humility.

All of the virtues mentioned in this section (compassion, kindness, humility, gentleness, patience, bearing with one another, and forgiveness) must come together under the banner of love, less they be deemed worthless. Nothing is more important to God than a husband's responsibility to love others. When Jesus said, "If you love me, feed my sheep" he wasn't just speaking to Peter, he was speaking to every man who would ever lay claim to loving God. No act perpetrated against a man will ever negate his responsibility to love. Even if a man's wife cheats on him, the responsibility to love still exists. Even if a man's wife disrespects him, the responsibility to love still exists. Even if a man's wife withholds affection from him, the responsibility to love still exists. Love is a constant within the husband's walk, and must be lived out each and every day of his life.

Chapter 5

A Husband's Marriage Responsibility

The Seven Main Responsibilities of a Husband

"Husbands, love your wives, just as Christ loved the church and gave himself up for her."

Ephesians 5:25

A husband is responsible for many things within his marriage. **First** and foremost, he is responsible for loving his wife, through the virtues set forth in Colossians 3:12-13 (compassion, kindness, humility, gentleness, patience, bearing with one another, and forgiveness). He must also love his wife in a manner that mirrors Christ's love for the church. This requires that the husband provide for his wife's daily needs, and offer himself to her sacrificially; laying his life down so that she might live.

Second, the husband is responsible for cleansing his wife by washing her with the word of God. That means speaking words of life over her, and affirming the promises that God has for her and the marriage collectively. **Third**, the husband is responsible for uniting with his wife and becoming one with her (spiritually, emotionally, and physically). The physical uniting between a husband and wife is called "sexual relations," which, in the context of marriage, is a duty that must not be withheld without mutual marital consent.

Fourth, the husband is responsible for keeping the relationship from any toxic or contaminating influences. This includes family, friends, children or even himself for that matter.

Fifth, the husband is responsible for understanding his wife and dwelling with her according to knowledge.

Sixth, the husband is responsible for fulfilling his wife's desire for intimacy by praying with (and for) her, conversing with her, and showering her with affection.

Seventh, the husband is responsible for remaining faithful to both his wife and the marriage covenant established by God (which the husband is part of by virtue of his marriage vow). The husband must realize that he is part of God's marriage covenant; and by transgressing against his wife he transgresses against God.

11 Key Marriage Principles for Husbands

There are eleven key marriage principles that a husband must own. These principles are tied to the seven fundamental marriage responsibilities listed in the preceding paragraphs. I urge husbands to meditate on these principles along with the insights that accompany them. Sow these principles deep into your Spirit, and be empowered as you fulfill God's plan for you as a husband.

MARRIAGE PRINCIPLE #1

Husbands and Wives are Created Differently.

"Haven't you read," he replied, "that at the beginning the Creator 'made them male and female'"

Matthew 19:4

Husband's Notes on Matthew 19:4

This is an important scripture to begin with because it lays the groundwork for everything that God will communicate about the marriage covenant in verses 5 and 6. A man leaving his father and mother, uniting to his wife, becoming one with her, guarding his marital union; all these things are premised upon the simple fact that "at the beginning the creator made them male and female."

When you think about it, it makes a lot of sense for God to say, "Before we even talk about covenant, before we even talk about leaving father and mother and joining together in holy matrimony, before we talk about oneness, intimacy, communication or any of these things, let's just understand this one very important thing, in the beginning I made men and women differently."

If a man tries to address the thought of leaving his father and mother and cleaving to his wife without first understanding that "*in the beginning the creator made them male and female*" he's going to find himself in a world of trouble. If a man tries to address the idea of "*what God has joined together, let man not separate*" without first understanding that "*in the beginning the creator made them male and female*" he'll find himself upset and frustrated. This phrase becomes the lens (second only to the Holy Spirit) through which a husband assesses every issue that he will encounter with his wife.

When a husband has difficulties communicating with his wife, one of the first things that should come to his mind is, "*in the beginning the creator made them male and female.*" If a husband is feeling rejected or ignored by his wife, one of the first things that should come to his mind is, "*in the beginning creator made them male and female."* If his wife won't respect him, or refuses to let him lead, one of the first things that should come to his mind is, *"in the beginning the creator made them male and female."* This is the foundational phrase that a husband uses to gain perspective, insight and understanding into his wife's world. If a man goes into a marriage operating on the premise that his wife thinks (or should think) the same way he does, he deceives himself, and invites stress into his marriage. Everything that the husband observes about his wife must be processed through the filter of *"In the beginning, the creator made them male and female."* In the end, almost everything reverts back to this truth.

Even today's scholars of biology and physiology finally have arrived at the conclusion that men and women are two uniquely different creations. A study at the University of California at Irvine uncovered that men and women use different sides of their brains to process and store long-term memories of emotional experiences. Through this study, it was discovered that the amygdala, an almond-shaped structure found on both sides of the brain, processes emotionally influenced memories exclusively on the right side of the brain in men and on the left side of the brain in women. The researchers also discovered that the amygdala secretes different levels of emotionally charged hormones in both men and women.

What does this all mean? It means that a husband and wife can witness the same exact event and recall it in two completely different ways. Why is that? It's because the emotionally charged hormone production levels in men and women differ, which means that the level of emotional attachment that men and women have towards certain events tend to differ as well. So the way man recalls an event might be markedly different from how a woman recalls it, simply because of the contrasting levels of emotional attachment to that particular event. Thus, a man can have an argument with his wife and be "somewhat" emotionally affected by it. But his wife can experience the same exact argument and be "emotionally devastated" by it. These emotional distinctions can make the husband appear insensitive or even aloof to his surroundings at times. But the reality is, "*in the beginning the creator made them male and female.*"

Another study released by The University of Pittsburgh described how men and women harbor different types of genes that impact susceptibility to depression. The study identified certain "sex-specific" genes for recurrent depression patterns among men and women, and concluded that not all depression is created equal. The genes that make a man susceptible to depression are different than the genes that make a woman susceptible to depression. This affects the way in which man and woman experiences depression, and more importantly, how their depression is treated.

What does this mean for the husband? Well, it essentially means that the husband must redefine how he views depression. He must realize that the things that make his wife susceptible to depression are likely different from what makes him susceptible to depression. The husband must also realize that how he goes about overcoming depression will likely be different from how his wife goes about it. For example, he may deal with his depression by sitting around the house and watching television. His wife however, may deal with her depression by getting out for some fresh air or maybe a little time out with her friends. One spouse handles their depression by removing themselves from the world, the other spouse handles their depression by going out and engaging themselves in the world; simply because of the differences in how each was created. These uniquely different approaches in handling depression can give rise to misunderstandings, criticisms and false judgments within a relationship, as both husbands and wives try and navigate through their pain. But at no point should the husband or wife be alarmed by these differences. They should instead embrace the reality that, "*In the beginning the creator made them male and female.*"

When a man says "I do" to a woman at the altar, he must realize that he's farther away from that woman (in likeness) than he can possibly know. It's the journey of oneness that reconciles the physiological, cultural, and experiential differences that exist between a husband and wife at the altar. A man must understand that he's a completely different specimen from the woman that he marries. Not only that, but he must also understand how those differences play a role in God's plan for marital oneness.

MARRIAGE PRINCIPLE #2

The Husband Must Detach from His Father and His Mother.

"For this reason a man will <u>leave his father and mother</u> and be united to his wife, and the two will become one flesh."

Matthew 19:5

Husband's Notes on Matthew 19:5

When I first read this scripture, I thought it had to do with man's transition away from dependence upon his family. It appeared to be telling the man to break away from his family ties; and not rely so heavily upon his parents the way he did when he was single. The man's "physical distancing" from his parental comfort zone seemed to be the focus in this scripture. But over the course of time I've come to realize that "physical distancing" in itself does not encompass the full context of this scripture. When the scripture says, "for this reason a man will leave his father and mother" it's not just talking about a man's physical departure from his parents. It's also talking about a man's symbolic departure from his "family identification." By family identification I'm talking about the "character DNA" that's branded and followed a man's family for generations.

Every family has its own identification. By this I mean, every family has its own unique traits that characterize it. These traits are so strong that they almost become synonymous with the family itself. It's hard to think about a family without thinking about the identification of that family. Whether it's the Kennedy family or the Kardashian family, there will always be certain traits or images that are associated with any given family. And those traits and images cannot be separated from that family's identification.

There are some family identifications that are good, and

some family identifications that are not so good. Good family identifications tend to edify and improve the quality of life for those within that family. Poor family identifications tend to diminish the quality of life for those within that family. In some families, verbal abuse is the family identification. So you'll find a great deal of volatile exchanges taking place among family members. These exchanges could come at a family reunion, a dinner table, or even a mall; it doesn't matter, it's the way that family operates. For them, it's the norm. In fact, where there are no volatile exchanges in effect, family members start to feel as if there's something wrong.

In some families, alcohol is the family identification. So whenever that family hosts a social event, you know there's going to be alcohol present. In fact, when there's no alcohol at a gathering, the family feels as if something is wrong. The family members actually believe that if there's no alcohol at the event, the event really isn't worth having. Alcohol is the family ID. The brothers do it, the father does it, the uncle does it; that's just how the family operates.

In some families, fighting is the family ID. These are the families that you know not to mess around with; because if you do, they'll get every person in the house to come out and fight you. Even the littlest of children in that household is a fighter. That is their family ID. **If a man carries the DNA of fighting, he'll bring a combative spirit into each and every relationship that he has.**

"The Argumentative Wife"

I know of a woman who came from a very argumentative household, in fact, that was her family's ID; arguing. If a person wanted to survive in that family, they had to know how to argue. So all this woman did growing up was argue with her siblings. Back and forth they went, no issue was too small for them to debate. And it wasn't that the arguments were mean-spirited. It was just the normal way that they communicated within the home.

Then one day this woman got married. And as quickly as she entered into her newly formed union, did she also bring the family ID of arguing along with her. However, little did this woman know that even as she brought the family ID of fighting into her newly formed marriage, her new husband was also in the process of bringing his own family ID into the marriage as well. And as things would have it, his family ID was completely different from her family ID. In his family ID, there was a culture of suppression, hiding, and avoiding issues.

Confrontation was avoided at all times. Arguments were an anomaly. In his family, combative discussions meant serious trouble.

So when these two family ID's came together, it produced the perfect storm. Almost every time this woman spoke to her husband, he was offended because he would always feel as if she was raising her voice at him. The wife on the other hand, would perceive her husband's quietness as weakness or indifference towards what was happening in the relationship.

Both the husband and wife were trying to assert a family ID that wasn't reflective of who they were as a collective couple. They needed to establish a "new family ID," one that expressed their collective ideals, personality and values as a united entity.

"The Resentful Son"

I know of a man who grew up despising his father. In fact, this man resented his father so much so that he would not even invite him to his wedding. Shortly after this man got married, he began having a lot of arguments with his new wife. For awhile, he had no idea why he was having such a hard time with her. But eventually, the man began to realize that his wife was not the issue, he was. He realized that he was living out a family identification that was passed down by his father. This family identification was rooted in critical and judgmental evaluations of others. It was an incredibly staunch and resolute ID anchored by pride. Unbeknownst to the man, he had embraced those same critical tendencies; and was now attempting to fuse them into his marriage. The man successfully kept his father from attending his wedding, but couldn't prevent him from taking up residency within his marriage.

In the end, this almost caused a marriage fatality. But by the grace of God, this man finally realized what was happening. By bringing dysfunctional DNA into his newly formed marriage, his marriage became a carrier of that DNA. The man knew that he couldn't allow this to happen. So he began the arduous process of purging certain character traits from his life, and detaching himself from his family ID, so that a new family ID could be birthed.

As I mentioned before, not all family ID's, are bad. There are some great family ID's that are absolutely worth fusing into a marriage. God simply calls the husband to detach himself from those family identifications that are unhealthy and unproductive, so that new family ID's can be established that are healthy, productive, and prosperous in nature.

Not only is it important for the husband to learn how to detach himself from unhealthy/unproductive family identifications, it's equally important for him to learn how to detach himself from the pain and emotion that's associated with those unhealthy identifications. It's hard for a man to detach himself from the pain and emotion connected to his family identification. This is something that he carries his entire life, and instinctively cleaves to, even if that identification causes him pain. Nevertheless, God is calling the husband to detach from that identification for his own good and the good of his new family. This is a responsibility that every husband has.

MARRIAGE PRINCIPLE #3

The Husband Must Unite With His Wife.

"For this reason a man will leave his father and mother <u>and be united to his wife</u>, and the two will become one flesh"

Matthew 19:5

Husband's Notes on Matthew 19:5

"Why God Unites a Man and a Woman"

God unites a man and woman together in holy matrimony because he wants to produce righteous offspring through them. It doesn't matter if it's the offspring of "children," the offspring of "mentees," the offspring of "a business," or the offspring of "a ministry;" God wants to righteously reproduce himself through the union of a man and a woman.

God doesn't just desire "any type of reproduction." God desires "righteous reproduction." If an unkind man and an unkind woman join together in holy matrimony and reproduce unkindness, this does not please God. If an abusive man and an abusive woman join together in holy matrimony and reproduce abuse, this does not please God. But if a loving man and loving woman join together in holy matrimony and reproduce love, it brings great pleasure to God, because a righteous purpose has been fulfilled through His union.

"Preparing For Righteous Reproduction"

God desires righteous fruit from the husband and wife relationship. This is why a single man works hard at developing his character fruit before he gets married. This is why all of his effort goes into building an intimate relationship with Christ while he is single. He's preparing himself for the reproductive process that's yet to come. He's preparing for the new identity to be birthed out of his marriage union. He realizes that whoever he is (in character) at the point he unites with his wife, will reproduce within the fabric of his marriage.

This is why a man must detach himself from unhealthy family identifications prior to entering the marriage covenant. This is why he has to let God free him from the prison of painful childhood memories prior to entering the marriage covenant. A man must carry with him to the marriage altar, a certain wholeness in character and spirit that's conducive for righteous reproduction.

If for some reason a man fails to work on his relationship with the Lord before he gets married, he shouldn't panic! The Lord can and will help him in developing spiritually over time so that he'll be ripe to reproduce in a way that glorifies God. During the first five years of marriage, his fruit may not look so promising (well, in my first five years, the fruit was just "bad"). But over the course of time, as that man grows spiritually in Christ, the fruit of his offspring will begin to look more and more like the one who created him.

"Unity Creates One Flesh"

Unity is the essential prerequisite for a husband and wife's righteous reproduction. Unity is the actual physical and spiritual joining that occurs between a husband and wife. The process is often called "becoming one flesh." Of all the marriage responsibilities, "uniting" is the one that most men like the best because of the "physical benefits" associated with joining together with a woman. But uniting (or becoming "one flesh") with a woman is more than just a physical action. It involves a series of integrated actions that links the mental, emotional, spiritual aspects of the human experience. Many of these links run deep and extend far beyond a man's ability to comprehend.

"The Absolute Commitment to Unify"

A man cannot unite with his wife at a "physical level" only; he must unite with her in a way that is "absolute." This requires an "absolute commitment" from him. An absolute commitment is a commitment that a husband makes to God. This is not a commitment that a man makes to his wife at the altar. The commitment that a man makes to his wife at the altar is conditional, subject to the laws that govern that particular state or land. When a husband or wife breaks the marriage commitment, the remedy for reconciliation is the law.

An absolute commitment (on the other hand) is a commitment that is made to God, not one's spouse. It's lifelong and all-inclusive. When a man breaks his absolute commitment to God, the remedy for reconciliation is the word of God. This is what makes marriage so special; it's an absolute commitment to God. And as such, the commitment is lifelong in that, it lasts as long as the two people within the marriage stay alive. It's also all-inclusive, in that it requires two completely different human beings to merge two entirely different lives into one.

"You Can't Reproduce from a Place of Separation"

Now this may sound obvious, but a man cannot reproduce with his wife from a place of separation. Nor can he become one with his wife from a place of separation. He must be joined unto his wife. Often times I've heard husbands say: "She has her money, I have my money." "She has her friends, I have my friends." "She has her hobbies, I have mine." "She has her family, I have mine." This is language of men who look to become one from a place of separation.

It sounds counterintuitive, but how can a man build from a place of separation and expect oneness in his marriage? How does he sow seeds of separation in his marriage and expect a harvest of oneness? A man should expect a harvest that is consistent with the seed he has sown. So if he sows separation into his marriage, he should not be surprised when separation surfaces within his marriage. If he sows unity into his marriage, he should not be surprised when unity surfaces within his marriage.

When a man builds alone, he builds from a place of separation. But when he builds collectively with his wife, he builds from a place of unity. Even our domestic relations laws are designed around this concept of "collective building." Whenever a couple divorces, their assets are divided among the two according to what they've "built collectively," in opposed to what they've built individually (before consummating the marriage). It's a legal presupposition that whatever a couple builds after they marry is built "collectively."

When a man builds his finances apart from his wife's finances, he is building his finances from a place of separation. When he builds his hobbies apart from his wife's hobbies, he builds from a place of separation. When he builds his goals apart from his wife's goals, he builds from a place of separation. If a husband's intent is to build from a place of separation, that's his choice; but he must understand that the fruit of his choice will be separation within his marriage.

MARRIAGE PRINCIPLE #4

The Husband Must Love His Wife.

"Husbands, love your wives, just as Christ loved the church and gave himself up for her."

Ephesians 5:25

Husband's Notes on Ephesians 5:25

At no point is a husband more Christ-like within his marriage than when he lays his life down for his wife. A man's love for his wife is not measured by how sentimental or emotional he is towards her. Nor is his love measured by how many beautiful and expensive gifts he gives to her. The husband's greatest demonstration of love towards his wife occurs when he dies in order to save her life. The book of John says "Greater love has no one than this: to lay down one's life for one's friends." (John 15:13) When a husband makes dying for his wife a habit, he makes love a habit as well.

The most practical expression of a life laid down is the voluntary assumption of another person's debt. When a man assumes his wife's debts as his own, he tells her that he's not only willing to identify with her weaknesses; he's willing to bear them as well.

It's easy for a husband to distance himself from his wife amidst her weakness. But God calls the husband to draw near to his wife in her weakness and bear her burdens upon himself. When a wife presents her burdens to her husband, he often gets frustrated because he feels like she's overwhelming him with "stuff." But the biblical model instructs the husband to take ownership of her burdens, so that he can then cast them upon the Lord (who owns all burdens). This is how the husband becomes Christ-like in the marriage; this is how he loves his wife the same way that Christ loves the church.

What does a husband's love towards his wife look like? Below are a few basic examples of how a husband lays down his life for his wife on a daily basis:

WAYS OF LAYING DOWN YOUR LIFE FOR YOUR WIFE

* Opening the car door for your wife and letting her in first before you enter is a form of laying down your life.	* Making sure that your wife has eaten and is fully satisfied before you begin eating is a form of laying down your life.
* Carrying heavy bags or heavy items so that your wife doesn't have to bear such a burden is a form of laying down your life.	* Saving your best energy for your wife is a form of laying down your life.
* Telling your wife that you love and appreciate her even while you are upset with her is a way of laying down your life.	* Apologizing to your wife when you don't feel like doing so is a form of laying down your life.

* Saying a cheerful "good morning" to your wife amidst early morning grogginess is a form of laying down your life.	* Satisfying your wife sexually before you satisfy yourself is a form of laying down your life.
* Resolving any outstanding household projects or duties that your wife has asked you to complete is a form of laying down your life.	* Pulling away from your favorite television program to address your wife's question (or questions) is a form of laying down your life.
* Helping your wife with child care and domestic responsibilities is a form of laying down your life.	* Working multiple jobs so that your wife can freely pursue her heart's desire is a form of laying down your life.
* Assuming any role in the home that's necessary in order to maintain functionality within that home is a form of laying down your life.	* Interrupting your daily work processes to think about your wife (as a blessing) is a form of laying down your life.

MARRIAGE PRINCIPLE #5

Spiritually Guard Yourself and Stay Connected your Wife.

"So guard yourself in your spirit, and do not break faith with the wife of your youth."

Malachi 2:15

Husband's Notes on Matthew 19:4

If we had to define the husband's two most significant day-to-day job responsibilities, it would be: (#1) "love" and (#2) "risk management." We've talked a lot about love up to this point in the book, but this scripture in Malachi 2 focuses on "risk management." Risk management is the study of any and all probability that wrongdoing might occur; and the use of effective measures to prevent such outcomes.

Malachi admonishes the husband to "guard himself" in spirit, and not to break faith with his wife. In other words, he's telling the husband that he must be in the business of risk management if he wants his spirit and marriage to live. He's saying (in no uncertain terms) that the husband must foresee those things that can potentially compromise his spirit, and guard himself against those things. As a job function, this is what a husband does each and every day of his life.

The risk manager has two main areas of focus: (1) guarding the integrity of the asset, and (2) increasing the asset's value. This is where the risk manager puts his all of his focus. He protects his asset at all times and consistently finds ways to increase its value. For the husband, his two greatest assets are his marriage to the Lord, and his marriage to his wife. No two assets in the husband's life are more significant than these.

As a risk manager, the husband must do three very important things in order to guard the integrity of his marriage asset. **First**, he must make choices and decisions that protect the asset's integrity. Every single decision that a husband makes will either reduce risk to his marriage asset or increase risk to it. From the very moment he wakes up in the morning, he must consider what decisions he will make that day that can potentially increase or decrease risk to his marriage asset. Whether it's a casual conversation with someone of the opposite sex during the daily commute, or going out with co-workers for happy hour after a long day's work; the decisions that a husband makes over the course of his day will most certainly increase or decrease risk to his marriage asset.

The **second** thing that a husband must do to guard the integrity of his marriage asset is understand his propensities and vulnerabilities. Every man has propensities and vulnerabilities. For example, some men have propensities for complaining. This type of man is highly vulnerable to situations and circumstances where complaints are in order. This man will always seem to attract poor service, or incompetent employees. There's always something to scrutinize for the man who has a propensity for complaining.

Some men have a propensity for overeating. This man is highly vulnerable to situations and circumstances where there's an abundance of food present (i.e. holidays, family gatherings, etc). Some men have a propensity for flirting, and become highly vulnerable to engage in this activity when compliments or attention is given to them by someone they admire. **A man's propensities/vulnerabilities can become a gateway into his life that can potentially compromise the integrity of his marriage asset. He must never lose sight of this.**

The last thing that a husband must do to guard the integrity of his marriage asset is evaluate the sights, sounds, and information he exposes himself to on a daily basis. The husband must think how these things may compromise the integrity of his marriage asset. Do the songs that he listens to compromise the integrity of his marriage asset? Do the images that he takes in compromise the integrity of his marriage asset? Does the information that he consumes compromise the integrity of his marriage asset? A husband must evaluate the sights, sounds and information that he's exposed to each and every day, and decide how these things can potentially compromise the integrity of his marriage asset. If at any point he feels like his marriage asset is at risk, he must reconsider whether or not he will continue to expose himself to that particular thing.

There are nine important practices that will help the husband reduce risk to his marriage asset. These practices are extrapolated from the Psalm 101 depiction of a man who lives "a blameless life." The scriptures says that the man who lives a blameless life submits himself to the following practices: (1) he lives a life of integrity (2) he protects his eyes (3) protects his heart (4) he separates himself from sin (5) he avoids covert insults (6) he avoiding pride (7) he ministers to God in his daily walk (8) he make a habit of being honest and truthful (9) and he cuts off all unrighteous relationships. When a husband engages these nine practices on a consistent basis, he not only diminishes risk to his marriage asset; he strengthens the asset's fortitude as well.

MARRIAGE PRINCIPLE #6

Remove any Intrusive or Divisive Influences.

"Therefore what God has joined together, let man not separate."

Matthew 19:5

Husband's Notes on Matthew 19:5

As part of the husband's role as risk manager, he must protect the value and integrity of the marriage asset. He does this in part by keeping intrusive or divisive influences away from his relationship. An "intrusive or divisive influence" by definition is any influence that fails to respect the boundaries of marriage covenant.

Wherever there are people in a man's life that have great needs and/or insecurities, there you will find a potentially divisive influence within his marriage. That divisive influence could be a friend, an associate, a family member, a sibling, a parent, a child, or even a ministry. Such an influence cannot be allowed to disrupt the fabric of a marriage. Matthew 19:5 tells us that it's God who ultimately unites a man and woman in holy matrimony. Therefore, no intrusive or divisive influence can ever be allowed to disrupt what God Himself has brought together.

It may sound strange, but the most divisive influence that exists within a marriage relationship is the husband and wife themselves. This is why a husband must first protect the marriage from himself before he does anything else. The more of him that's infused into his marriage, the greater the risk of failure his marriage will have. Conversely, the more of Christ that's infused into his marriage, the lower the risk of failure his marriage will have.

MARRIAGE PRINCIPLE #7

Do Not Divorce Your Wife.

"And a Husband Must Not Divorce His Wife."

1 Corinthians7:10

Husband's Notes on 1 Corinthians 7:10

In the first part of this scripture, God tells the wife not to separate from her husband. The word "separate" there is "chōrizō," which means to depart or "go away." In the following scripture, God tells the husband not to divorce his wife. The Greek word used for divorce here is "aphiēmi," which means "to put away." The image here is of someone physically putting away an object, or physically removing a particular thing from their presence.

In essence, God tells the wife not to separate from her husband, while telling the husband not to divorce his wife. The fact that God distinguishes between separation ("going away") and divorce ("putting away") is profound, because in those times, women were not allowed to make formal divorce petitions against their husbands. Husbands had to "let their wives go." Conversely, wives had to literally "run away" from their husbands if they wanted to end their marriage. So this created a norm where husbands were more inclined to "put away" their wives, while wives were more inclined to "go away" from their husbands.

God's commanding the husband not to "put away" his wife, while commanding the wife not to "go away" from her husband, is profound in more ways than one. The wording actually speaks to the differences in how men and women handle relationship conflict. For example, if you examine the conflict resolution styles of both men and women, you'll find that each has a unique approach towards handling these types of matters.

For example, if a man is hurt by his wife, his first tendency will be to try and physically remove her from his presence. Why is that? Well, a man instinctively rejects those things that are heavy, hurtful or burdensome to him, so if something comes into his life that represents one of these three things, he'll try and physically remove that thing from his presence. On the other hand, if a wife is hurt by her husband, her first inclination will be to mentally and emotionally distance herself from him. Unlike the husband, the wife's pain is not driven by her heaviness, hurt or burden brought on by the situation. Her pain is driven by feeling unloved, unwanted, or insignificant in the eyes of her husband. These things cause a wife to distance herself from her husband.

It's important to note that a wife's distancing from her husband first takes place in the mental, emotional and spiritual realm, before moving into the physical. That's why a woman mentally and emotionally departs from a man long before she physically leaves him; but a man physically leaves a woman long before he mentally and emotionally departs from her.

God addresses two different individuals within the context of this scripture. He addresses the husband who wants to physically remove his wife out of his life; and He addresses the wife who wants to mentally and emotionally distance herself from her husband. God knows the individual tendencies of both husband and wife, and He takes the opportunity to speak to those unique tendencies through this scripture.

MARRIAGE PRINCIPLE #8

Don't Divorce Your Non-Believing Wife If She Wants To Stay.

"If a brother has a wife who is not a believer and she is willing to live with him, he must not divorce her."

1 Corinthians 7:13

Husband's Notes on 1 Corinthians 7:13

One of the first acts of power that God demonstrated in the bible was the separation of light from darkness. It was here that he first declared that the light "was good." (Genesis 1:4) From that point on in the scriptures, God identifies with the light in a very unique and personal way. In John 8:12 Jesus refers to himself as "the light of the world." He goes on to say that if anyone chooses to follow Him, they will not walk in darkness but have the "light of life." In John 1:4 John refers to Jesus as the "life" that represents the "light" to all mankind. God uses light as a boundary line to distinguish those who follow Him from those who do not. For those that do not follow Him, they remain in darkness. But for those that do follow Him, they are called, "Children of Light." (Ephesians 5:8)

Darkness can only be overcome by the light of God's glory, Jesus Christ. (2 Corinthians 4:6) The belief and acceptance of the light creates "the newbirth." Jesus said that until a man experiences this newbirth "he cannot see" the Kingdom of God. (John 3:3) John 3:20 says that everyone born of darkness hates the light. That implicitly means that those in the dark have an innately contentious disposition towards those who are in the light.

The bible says that a child of light should not be "yoked" (or bound) to one who lives in darkness. (2 Corinthians 6:14) Simply put, a believer should not be intimately attached to an unbeliever. When a believer intimately attaches himself to a non-believer, it gives darkness legal right to inhabit the light. Not only does this potentially dilute the light inside of the believer, but depending on how influential the darkness is, it can also jeopardize the life of the believer as well.

There are some life situations in life where a believer may find himself married (or yoked) to an unbeliever. The believer may have accepted salvation after they got married, or maybe they heard the 2nd Corinthians admonition, but still made the decision to marry anyway. Regardless of how the situation came to pass, the believer is now confronted with the responsibility of becoming one with a spouse who resides in darkness. They have to communicate things pertaining to the Kingdom of God, with a mate who cannot see the Kingdom, nor understand it. They have to share spiritual insights with a spouse who sees the Word of God as foolishness. (1st Corinthians 2:13) And to top it all off, they must do all of these things while their spouse despises the light that is in them (John 3:20).

God is acutely aware of every potential challenge that a believing husband has in being married to non-believing wife. Nevertheless, God still declares that the marriage covenant remain intact if a non-believing wife wants to stay with her believing husband. God declares that a marriage between a darkness and light can succeed if enough light shines in that relationship to overcome darkness. In the same way God said "let there be light" at the beginning of creation, and light was birthed amidst darkness, is the same way that God sends the believing spouse into a marriage as a beacon of light to shine brightly amidst the darkness of that unbelieving spouse's heart.

It's inevitable that spiritual conflicts will arise between a believing husband and non-believing wife. But God's light has the power to overcome darkness. 2 Samuel 22:29 says, "You Lord you are my lamp; the Lord turns my darkness into light." Ephesians 5:8 (NASB) says "for you were formerly darkness, but now you are Light in the Lord; walk as children of Light." These scriptures reveal to us that there is hope for the marriage that is unevenly yoked; if only for the fact that someone in that marriage is walking in the light. 1st Corinthians 7:14 says that an unbelieving husband is actually "sanctified" (or set apart) simply because of the marital connection to his believing wife. I happen to be convinced that the believing husband also sanctifies the wife in the same way. That's the power of the marriage covenant. That's the power that God has to transfer a relationship from darkness into light.

The power of God's light and love within the marriage covenant supersedes even the most complex issues that arise between a believing husband and a non-believing wife. If an unbelieving wife wants to stay married to her believing husband, that husband should honor her wish. Instead of focusing on their spiritual differences, he should instead focus on being that child of light; representing Christ through his day-to-day unconditional love walk with her.

MARRIAGE PRINCIPLE #9

Honor Your Marriage by Making Intimacy Pure and Exclusive.

"Marriage should be honored by all, and the marriage bed kept pure, for God will judge the adulterer and all the sexually immoral."

Hebrews 13:4

Husband's Notes on Hebrews 13:4

The word "honor" seems to be somewhat of an outdated phrase; only used in areas such as the military, law enforcement and education. But seldom do we see honor referenced as a practice in today's marriages. **To honor something means that "you highly esteem it, passionately cherish it, and greatly value it."** You don't honor a thing through one single action. You honor a thing through a series of thoughts and actions that collectively demonstrate reverence for a particular thing.

Secondly, honor is not something that is given based on comprehensive merit. In other words, we don't look at someone's life in totality and assess whether or not they deserve honor. Honor is something that is given based on two basic things; position and achievement. That boils the test for honor down to one simple question, "does the position or achievement warrant honor?" If the position warrants honor, then we honor the position, no questions asked. If the achievement warrants honor, then we honor the achievement, no questions asked.

When we give someone honor, we're really honoring the position or achievement rather than the individual person. That's a hard pill for many of us to swallow, because in our minds we want honorable people to warrant honor in every area of their life, not just the area that we honor them for. It breaks our heart when we find someone that we've honored living dishonorably in other areas of their life. It breaks our heart to know that someone honored for their outstanding public service lives dishonorably in the area of marriage and family. It breaks our heart to know that someone honored for their great business acumen lives dishonorably in the area of personal integrity and morality. There will always be honorable people that have dishonorable aspects of their lives. But that doesn't prevent us from honoring their position or achievement. Ultimately, honor is all about revering the position and achievement, not the individual who acquires these things.

The bible refers to honor as something that should be given "when it is due." (Romans 13:7) That means when honor is "due," it needs to be disbursed automatically, without thought or hesitation. Honor cannot be disbursed based upon our own personal views about an individual, nor can it be disbursed based upon how we feel about certain dishonorable areas within a person's life. God removes the "likeability factor" from the honor analysis, and boils things down to a simple "if/then statement." If honor is due, then give it. If someone holds an honorable position, then honor that position. God wants us to dispel honor with absoluteness; especially within the area of marriage and family.

Hebrews 13:4, says that marriage should be honored by "all." That means that a man must highly esteem, passionately cherish, and greatly value his marriage. In fact, one of the greatest safeguards that a man has to prevent a failed marriage is honor. Honor within a marriage is powerful because it's not just an isolated activity; it's an ongoing, seamless thread within the fabric of a marriage. If a man takes his wife out to celebrate their anniversary for one night, and ignores his marriage for the remainder year, he has not honored his marriage. Don't get me wrong, he has done a noble thing by taking his wife out, and should be acknowledged for his noble act. But he has not demonstrated honor in the truest sense of the word. A husband demonstrates honor within his marriage when he cherishes it each and every day. He honors his marriage when he thinks about his wife and the things that bring value to his relationship with her. He honors his marriage when he meditates on the positive aspects of his relationship and prays for wisdom in those areas that need improvement. A husband honors his marriage when he, as a risk manager, makes choices and decisions that protect the value of his marriage asset. This is the type of honor gives a marriage longevity.

The second part of Hebrews 13:4 tells the husband to keep the marriage bed "pure." Among other things, "purity" within the context of this scripture means that the husband must make intimacy within his marriage "exclusive." In relational terms we call this, "the power of exclusivity."

When a husband and wife makes the marriage covenant "exclusive," (that meaning God, the Husband, and the wife only) the marriage is kept pure. It doesn't matter whether it's exclusivity within conversations, or exclusivity within sexual relations, a marriage is kept pure to the degree that relations within that marriage are kept between God, the husband and the wife. Things such as extramarital affairs, pornography, inappropriate conversations/touching, flirtation, and sexual fantasies involving other parties, are all things that rob a marriage of its exclusiveness; which consequently robs a marriage of its purity. The more intimate a man becomes with things and people outside of his marriage, the more purity he extracts from the life of his marriage.

Purity is an issue of the heart. So when a man desires to be intimate with people outside of his marriage, it must be seen as a heart issue. Matt 15:19 says, "For out of the heart comes evil thoughts, murder, adultery, sexual immorality, theft, false testimony, slander." These are the issues of the heart that destroy purity within a marriage.

Flirtation is a heart condition that causes a man to exhibit emotionally and physically suggestive behavior towards someone that he either finds attractive, or he wants to appear attractive to. A husband's flirtation strips a marriage of its exclusiveness because it tells someone other than his wife, "you appeal to me." And by telling someone other than his wife, "you appeal to me," his wife no longer is uniquely appealing in his eyes. She must now share her husband with someone else who has captured his eye. Thus, the purity of "you appeal to me" no longer exists, and the wife loses her exclusiveness within the marriage.

"Marriage must be honored and the marriage bed kept pure." When a man honors his marriage, he highly esteems it, passionately cherishes it, and greatly values it. He does what is necessary to protect his marriage and increase its value. **He works hard at guarding his heart against any impurities that may potentially defile the sexual experiences he has with his wife.** There can never be an "anything goes" mentality in the bedroom. There must always be a spiritual check against any and all things that attempt to enter that very intimate space between a husband and a wife. If images and philosophies from movies, television, books, magazines, and the internet pervade a man's heart, it's going to unquestionably spill over into his sexual experience with his wife. **When a husband guards his spiritual diet and keeps ungodly influences out of his bedroom, he honors his marriage and keeps it pure and exclusive.**

MARRIAGE PRINCIPLE #10

Honor Your Wife's Right of Access to Your Body.

"The Husband should fulfill his marital duty to his wife, and likewise the wife to her husband."

1 Corinthians 7:3

Husband's Notes on 1 Corinthians 7:3

Sex in the bible is referred as a "responsibility." In 1 Corinthians 7:3 it says that "The husband should fulfill his marital duty to his wife, and likewise the wife to her husband." In Deuteronomy 24:5 it says that a man should not have any other duty laid upon him within his first year of marriage aside from his "marital duties." The scripture actually says that "for one year the husband is to be free to **stay at home and bring** 'happiness' to the wife he has married." One of the ways that a man brings happiness to his wife is by pleasing her sexually.

In 1 Corinthians 7:4 it states that "The wife does not have authority over her own body but yields it to her husband." It goes on to say that, "In the same way, the husband does not have authority over his own body but yields it to his wife." Now we often tend to think about this scripture within the context of sex, but if we look at this from a broader context, the bible is saying that the wife's body belongs to the husband, and the husband's body belongs to the wife. That means that **the husband and wife are both "mutually responsible" for how they take care of one another's body**. When a husband ministers to his wife's body, he is honoring his responsibility before God. When a wife ministers to her husband's body, she is honoring her responsibility before God. A man has a vested interest in how well his wife's body is maintained, because his wife's body belongs to him, and his body belongs to her.

If my wife asks me to go get a check-up, or if she gently encourages me to eat healthier, she honors her biblical responsibility to take care of her body; because my body belongs to her. And if I encourage my wife to live and eat healthy, or I encourage her to go to the doctor, I'm honoring my biblical responsibility as a husband, because I'm vested in the well being of her body. When a husband is constantly worn down and lacking energy/vitality, it affects the quality of his marriage. A husband must understand that he is "one" with his wife, and in that oneness he has the responsibility to not only give his body to his wife, but to care for his body as well. Husbands must make sure that they esteem and cherish their wives' right of access to their body. He must honor her by taking care of himself physically so that he can meet her physical needs the best way he can.

MARRIAGE PRINCIPLE #11

Be Considerate to Your Wife, and Treat Her With Respect.

"Husbands, in the same way be considerate as you live with your wives, and treat them with respect as the weaker partner and as heirs with you of the gracious gift of life, so that nothing will hinder your prayers."

1 Peter 3:7

Husband's Notes on 1 Peter 3:7

1 Peter 3:7 tells the husband to be "considerate" towards his wife as he lives with her. A considerate husband is one that is mindful of his wife's well being. He's a man who constantly thinks about his wife and how he can support her through his prayers, his time, his talent, and his treasury. A considerate husband thinks about the choices that he makes and how they will impact his wife's life.

A considerate husband is also one who is compassionate. We stated earlier in the book that compassion by definition is "when a husband identifies with and is sensitive to his wife's hurt, pain, need or plight." A husband's compassion brings him closer to his wife's issues. A husband cannot distance himself from his wife's issues and still be compassionate towards her. He must roll up his sleeves and get intimately involved with her struggles.

The second part of 1 Peter 3:7 instructs husbands to show respect towards their wives. Respect, like honor is something that righteously acknowledges an individual's God-given position or achievement. It's not a merit-based offering. When it's due, it's due, regardless of how you feel about the person that you're giving it to. In the same way, a man's respect for his wife must be given simply because the bible says "it is due," not because she does anything special to merit it. Some men feel that they should only respect their wives when they themselves are treated well by them. If this was the standard, some husbands could go on for years without any respect for their wives. But the bible says that respect is something that we extend to our wives not because of their conduct, but because of the God-given position that they hold as wives. Similarly, a wife should respect her husband, not because of how great he is, but because of the God-given position that he occupies as a husband.

The latter part of 1 Peter 3:7 examines the nexus between a man's respect for his wife and the efficacy of his prayers. Here, the husband is told to treat his wife with respect "as an heir of the gracious gift of life so that nothing will hinder his prayers." The intriguing thing about this statement is that it implies prayer to be a common function within the husband's life. This is not a foreign concept in the bible, as we've seen praying husbands on display on numerous occasions. In Genesis 25:21 Isaac prayed to the LORD on behalf of his wife Rebekah because she was childless. The LORD answered his prayer, and his wife became pregnant (with Jacob and Esau). In Luke 1:13 Zechariah prayed for his wife Elizabeth because she was childless, and the Lord dispatched an angel to let him know that his prayer had been heard, and would be fulfilled though the birth of a son named John. And finally, we see the greatest husband ever (Jesus) praying for his wife (the church) that she may be "one with Him" even as He and the Father are one - The Father in Him and Him in the Church.

A husband's prayers for his wife should be as common as the air that he breathes; and effective to the degree that he treats his wife with consideration and respect.

Chapter 6

A Husband's Oneness

A Husband Must Join Unto His Wife

"For this reason a man will leave his father and mother and be united to his wife, and the two will become one flesh. So they are no longer two, but one flesh. Therefore what God has joined together, let no one separate."

Mark 10:7-10

"The Six Essential Areas of Joining"

Ultimately, God desires righteous offspring from the marriage union. And in order for this to occur, a husband and wife must first be "joined". This section will highlight six areas that are essential to a husband's ability to join his wife.

(#1) AREA OF JOINING: FAITH

The first area that a husband must join his wife is the area of faith. A husband must put aside time to communicate the Word of God to his wife. He must wash her with the word of God each and every day. He does this in many ways, but first and foremost he does this by telling his wife what the Word of God says about her. When a man tells his wife that "she's more than a conqueror" (Romans 8:37) he washes her with the word. When he tells her she's given him the favor of God (Proverbs 18:22) he washes her with the word. When a husband washes his wife with the Word of God, he "joins" her in faith.

Another way that a man joins his wife in the area of faith is by sharing the promises that God has for their relationship. A Husband must be able to understand and articulate the promises that God has for his wife and their marriage. He must talk about the vision that God has, not just for himself, but for his wife as well. Many husbands don't pursue an understanding of where God is taking their wife, nor do they take a passionate interest in those things God has made her passionate about. **A husband can sometimes be so busy pursuing his own God-given dreams, that he overlooks the dreams that God has given to his wife.** When a man understands and becomes vested in his wife's God-given dreams, he combines his faith with hers, draws closer to her in the process.

A husband must tap into the God-given dream that's

deposited within his wife's heart. He must speak words of faith into her hearing each and every day, to encourage her as she progresses through some of life's most difficult challenges. He must remind her of the promises that God has for her and for their marriage as a whole. He must remind her of who she is in Christ, and more importantly, who she will become in Christ tomorrow, and in years to com. This is the way a husband joins his wife in the area of faith.

(#2) AREA OF JOINING - COMMUNICATION

The second area that a husband must join his wife is in the area of communication. People tend to measure effective communication by how well a person speaks. So when a man articulates himself well, we call him "a good communicator." We instinctively associate his good talking with an effectively communicated message. However, good articulation is not the litmus test for an effectively communicated message. An effectively communicated message is based on how well a man connects with the people he is trying to reach. **Thus, communication must be measured, not by a man's ability to talk, but by his ability to connect with others around him.**

"Connectivity = Communication"

When we use the phrase "joining in the area of communication," We're referring to how well a man connects with his wife. And by "connecting," we mean how well a man integrates into his wife's world, and how astute he is at understanding her likes, dislikes, needs, wants, and desires.

In order for a husband to effectively connect with his wife, he must establish lines of connectivity that integrate him into her world. He must find creative ways to not only establish lines of connectivity, but also ensure that those lines remain healthy and intact.

"Quality Lines = Quality Connectivity"

When we have difficulties accessing the internet, one of the first things we do is check the lines of connectivity. We check to see if the Wi-Fi networks are intact. We check to see if the website or server is down. We check to see if the DSL cable is up and running properly. We immediately identify the lines of connectivity as the source of failed communication. And so it is with marriage. When we encounter a problem with communication, the first thing that we must check is the lines of connectivity into our spouse's heart. We must find out if there's a connection problem. And if there's an issue, what must we do to re-establish the connection?

Establishing lines of connectivity to your wife's heart is absolutely critical to effective communication with her. But that's only part of what's required for effective communication. The other part of effective communication involves maintaining the health and well-being of those lines that you establish. If a man sets up lines of connectivity to his wife's heart, but doesn't think about how to keep those lines healthy and operable, he'll end up with many lines of connectivity, but with no functionality. The same goes for communication in a marriage. A man can build tremendous gateways into his wife's world; he can spend quality time with her, take her to her favorite restaurants, go shopping with her, and even shower her with gifts. But if he's rude, condescending, judgmental, and complaining at the same time, his communication towards her will be no more effective than a large, inoperable fiber optics network. He's got all the lines of connectivity, and is poised to integrate with his wife, but his attitude corrodes the lines, which makes his communication towards her ineffective.

A husband who has strong, integrated lines of connectivity into his wife's heart doesn't need great articulation. In fact, there are times when a man doesn't need to articulate one single word in order to effectively communicate with his wife. Sometimes he just connects through a caring look, a smile, or a gentle rubbing of his wife's hands. Through these seemingly insignificant gestures, everything that the husband wants to say is already communicated.

"Connecting Through Language"

A man doesn't need great articulation in order to effectively communicate with his wife. But when he does articulate, he must do so in a language that his wife understands. Genesis11:1-9 teaches us that there are two basic things that happen when language breaks down between individuals in a relationship. **The first thing that happens** is that parties stop building together. Common language is a motivator for collaboration and a bridge to understanding. When that connector disappears, the tendency is for parties to discontinue their collaborative building. **The second thing that happens** is that the individuals go their separate ways. When two individuals no longer share the common connector of language, they experience a powerful sense of detachment that causes them to search for those connections in other places.

These two outcomes also hold true in a marriage whenever there's a disconnect within the area of language. If a husband cannot speak to his wife in a language she can understand, communication with her will inevitably break down. From there, two things are likely to happen. First, the husband and his wife will stop building together. Second, they will each go their separate ways. This doesn't necessarily mean that they'll divorce. It simply means that they're likely to go on living separate lives, as they gravitate towards those people and relationships that they can connect with. For example, if a husband loves football, but his wife wants nothing to do with it, he will separate from his wife in that particular area, and find someone who will speak the language of football with him. So they will not build as a couple in this area, but rather go their separate ways. Similarly, if a wife likes photography, but her husband dislikes it, she will look for someone who can speak the language of photography with her. The result once again is that the couple does not build in that particular area, and ultimately ends up going their separate ways.

When my wife made the decision to return to school in pursuit of her master's degree, I knew that she would be entering a completely different world. I knew that I had to make a decision whether or not I was going to be a passive supporter, or an active, integrally involved supporter in that new world. After thinking long and hard about the concept of language, connectivity and integration, I made the decision to go full-force into this new world along with my wife. Yes, she was the student, but I was going to make sure that I was a student as well. I wanted to have a "basic familiarity" with the things that she was studying. Like a classmate, I wanted to be able to connect with my wife when she finished her classes for the day.

As the school year began, I quietly began reading many of the books that my wife was assigned. The more I read, the more familiar I became with the things she was learning. Soon I was able to converse with my wife about things like cognitive behavior, passive-aggression, codependency, and classical conditioning. I was able to talk with her about the theories of Freud, and BF Skinner. I developed a relationship with the things that were close to my wife's heart. And in doing so, I formed a connector with her that integrated me into her world. I had succeeded at joining my wife in the area of communication.

(#3) AREA OF JOINING: EMOTIONS

The third area that a husband must join his wife is in the area of emotions. In order for a husband to join his wife emotionally, he must adjust his emotions in a way that connects with her. But how does a man adjust his emotions? It sounds really hard, but it's actually something that a man does each and every day.

A man's natural inclination is to mirror the behavior that's presented to him. So if someone greets him with a warm "hello," he's likely to respond in-kind with a warm greeting. If he's greeted rather lethargically, he may become a bit sluggish or lukewarm in his response. If he's greeted rudely, he may respond somewhat curtly or abruptly. These are all subtle adjustments that a man makes to his emotions on a daily basis. When a man identifies the correct emotional context, he responds in a way that's emotionally suitable. That's why he emotes differently at a funeral then he does at a wedding. That's why he emotes differently at a library than he does at a party. As the emotional landscape changes, so does the emotional expression for each situation.

There's no doubt that a man can, and will make the necessary emotional adjustments in order to connect with the world around him. But the question is, "how willing is he to make those same adjustments in order to connect with his wife?" The answer to this question will reveal just how effective that man is at "joining his wife emotionally."

What should a man do when his wife expresses her emotions in ways that are unpleasing or unbecoming to him? Should he get upset? Should he try and tell his wife how wrong she is for expressing herself in such a way? A man's goal should not be to tell his wife how wrong her emotions are. **His goal should always be to connect with her in the place that she emotionally resides at that very moment.** He must figure out the context of his wife's expression and connect with her in a way that's emotionally suitable.

Does this mean that a man must mirror every emotion that his wife displays? No, not at all. If a man's wife has an emotional meltdown, he should not mirror that emotion with his own meltdown. If she's depressed, he shouldn't mirror that emotion and become depressed. What he should do is make the necessary emotional adjustments in order to connect with his wife in her state of depression. The husband should not look to become his wife; he must look to create *a line of connectivity* that will allow him enter her emotional world with grace and sensitivity. He must look to adjust himself and his emotions in ways that reflect both his care and concern for his wife.

The ultimate goal for the husband is to be a light for his wife as she works through her emotional challenges. He must identify his wife's emotional landscape and direct his emotional output accordingly. Romans 12:15 tells a man to, "rejoice with those who rejoice and mourn with those who mourn." When a man engages his wife in such a way, he tells her, "I am with you", I share in your hurt, and I share in your joy. This is how a husband successfully joins his wife in the area of emotions.

(#4) AREA OF JOINING: SEXUAL RELATIONS

The fourth area that a husband must join his wife is the area of sexual relations. Sex occurs in a marriage when a husband and wife physically join their bodies together as one. This joining is the tangible expression of the spiritual union birthed through the marriage covenant. It takes both the physical and spiritual union to paint a complete picture of marital oneness. Without the physical union, the spiritual union lacks tangible evidence to support its existence. Without the spiritual union, the physical union is rendered shallow and void of any depth or substance.

God's purpose for sex is threefold: (1) to serve as a consummating instrument of the marriage covenant (2) to represent the physical symbol of the spiritual union between a husband and wife, and (3) to reproduce righteous offspring. So when a man has sex with a woman outside the parameters of marriage covenant, he distorts God's purpose for joining a man and a woman together, and perverts the very essence of sex.

One of the residual effects of sex is "bonding." God made bonding a part of the sexual experience so that a man could join his wife at a physiological level. During the act of sex there are certain hormones released that create bonds between the two parties engaged in the activity. Even if a man has sex with a prostitute, he still forms an inseparable bond with her that lasts well beyond their sexual encounter. The book of 1st Corinthians explains it this way, "Do you not know that he who unites himself with a prostitute is one with her in body? For it is said, 'The two will become one flesh.'" (1 Corinthians 6:16) The purpose that God has for joining a man and a woman together is uniquely tied to the purpose that God has for the marriage union. And when sex is engaged for purposes aside from these, it creates ties between individuals that were never meant to be tied, and reduces sex to nothing more than a mere act of pleasure.

When a husband and wife join sexually, it represents the physical glue that keeps the spiritual union intact. This glue is made of a powerful compound called "intimacy." Intimacy is what makes sex substantive. It's what makes sex meaningful. Without intimacy, sex is nothing more than a series of self-gratifying actions. With intimacy, sex becomes the crowning glory for the ultimate act of oneness.

The word intimacy comes from the latin word "intimatus", which means "closely_acquainted, or very familiar." Intimatus is derived from two words, "intimare" which means "to make known," and intimus which means "inmost, deepest within, or farthest from the external surface. When we look these three words in totality, we discover that the true meaning of intimacy resides in getting to know, or becoming acquainted with the innermost part of a person. This definition is consistent with the definition Jesus gave in John 15:15 when he said to the disciples, "I no longer call you servants, because a servant does not know his master's business. Instead, I have called you friends, for everything that I learned from my Father I have made known to you." Jesus defines the relationship with His disciples based on the depth and quality of information that he shares with them. In other words, the more information Jesus shared with His disciples, the more intimate he became with them.

A husband does not achieve a deep level of intimacy with his wife just because he knows everything about her. A husband can run a complete background check on his wife, and study every detail there is to know about her, and still lack intimacy with her. **A man becomes intimate with his wife, not just by knowing her ways, but by sharing his innermost self with her.** The highest levels of intimacy between a husband and wife are achieved through the sharing process. This occurs when a man makes an intentional decision to give of himself in a way that causes the barriers of formality and distance (between him and his wife) to come tumbling down. It's no surprise that some of the most intimate times within a couple's relationship occur at the beginning of their relationship, as the couple gets to know one another by sharing intimate details about themselves. Sometimes this sharing goes on for hours and hours via phone, internet, or in person. This is the time in a couple's relationship where they are most prone to giving their heart, mind and emotion to each other. This is the point where they are most ripe for intimacy.

Sex does not make a couple intimate. Sex is simply one of the bonding agents in the glue of intimacy. It's the exclusive, innermost sharing between a husband and wife that authenticates a couple's intimacy. Some men struggle with intimacy because they're too afraid to let their wives see their weakest and most vulnerable areas. They instead opt to conceal their weaknesses, which then mortgages intimacy with their wives. This puts a lien against the marriage that cannot be released until the husband's insecurities are fully reconciled.

On the other hand, if a man submits his insecurities to the Lord, he removes the intimacy lien against his marriage, and becomes free to share with his wife in more profound ways. This removes the barrier of intimacy within the man's marriage, and paves the way to joining in the area of sexual relations.

(#5) AREA OF JOINING: DAILY ACTIVITIES

The fifth area that a husband must join his wife is in daily activities. I know this sounds obvious, but a husband must spend time with his wife in order to join her. And with only 86,400 seconds in a single day, there's not a lot of time that a husband has to join his wife before a new day begins. Studies show that 81% of our time revolves around one of three daily activities: sleep, work, or watching television. So, if a man wants to successfully join his wife, he's going to have to be skillful in joining her at one (or all) of these activities.

(5a) "Join Your Wife When She Goes to Bed"

A man joining his wife as she goes to bed is very important. In fact, it's so important that I might go as far as to say that his entire schedule could revolve around this critical juncture in her day. When a wife goes to bed, her body is as close to being at peace as it will have been all day. The physical, mental, and emotional demands upon her are finally coming to a grinding halt. This should be the time in her day when she puts down her guard and joins her husband in peace, free from the stressors and complications of life. It's probably one of the few times in the day where a husband has the opportunity to join his wife across several planes (spiritual, mental, emotional, and physical). It's also a time in the day when a husband has the opportunity to set the stage for how well his wife sleeps during the night. A husband can actually help his wife usher in a peaceful night's sleep by affirming her with calming words, prayers, and promises that God has for her and their marriage. When a man does these things he "washes his wife with the Word of God." With so much on the line, it's certainly worth it for a man to try and rearrange his schedule to ensure that he's there with his wife during this critical point in her day.

What if a man and wife have completely different work schedules? How can a husband and wife join each other before they go to bed? This does create somewhat of a challenge, but I wouldn't say that this automatically prohibits a man from joining his wife at bedtime. With today's technologies, we now have the ability to communicate in a multitude of ways, despite the barriers of distance. Texting, phone calls, video streaming, Skype, and FaceTime are just a few of the ways that a husband can employ meaningful conversations with his wife at the time she goes to bed. Technology helps the husband overcome barriers of distance caused by conflicting work schedules.

(5b) "Join Your Wife During Her Work Day"

During the work day, the husband's first responsibility is to focus on the job at hand. However, that doesn't prelude us from taking a moment to think positively about our wives over the course of the day. It may just be a quick thought about something nice that your wife did during the week, or maybe something that she does all the time. No matter what type of positive thought it is, the most important thing is that you've made time to think about your wife in a positive way over the course of the day; and that's a big step towards joining her!

As you make time to think positively about your wife over the course of your work day, also think about how those thoughts can be converted into tangible actions when you arrive home. For example, a pleasant thought about your wife during the work day could become a "hug" when you get home, if for no other reason than to tell your wife, "I appreciate you." The overall goal is to make your workday relationship with your wife a "bridge" to intimacy for your return home. For most married couples, the workday does not operate as a bridge to intimacy; but rather an "island" that creates further distance between the husband and wife during the day.

As an exercise, take a few moments each day to give your wife a phone call, a text, an email or even a surprise lunch visit (if your schedule permits). It may be awkward at the beginning, but over the course of time, the intimacy bridge will eventually develop. If you decide not to establish this bridge, you'll have to start from scratch when you return home from work. I assure you, a few positive thoughts over the course of an 8 hour day, or even a 2 minute phone call, will not compromise the integrity of your job responsibilities in any way. In fact, studies show that the happier a man is in his marriage, the more likely he is to perform well in his place of employment.

(5c) "Join Your Wife When She Watches Television"

The Bureau of Labor Statistics states that the average American spends 2.8 hours a day watching television. That means that out of the 86,400 seconds in your wife's day, 10,080 seconds are spent in front of a television screen. By ignoring this activity, you could be potentially ignoring upwards of 12% of your wife's waking day.

A husband has a unique opportunity to bond with his wife by watching television with her. However, this bonding opportunity presents just as many potential challenges as it does potential blessings. Some men just don't like to watch television, or avoid watching television with their wives because they lack interest in the shows their wives watch. The choice to refrain from television is completely understandable, and in many cases, is the right thing to do. But even as he refrains, I would encourage him to still think about some creative ways to bond with his wife, even as she watches her favorite program.

For the man who refrains from watching television with his wife because he dislikes the shows that she watches, there are a few questions he should ask himself. The first question is, "will this program hurt my spiritual growth and development if I watch it?" If it will in fact hurt his spiritual development, he should not watch that program (no questions asked). He should instead take that time that he would have spent with his wife watching television, and devote it towards something that would help his wife prepare for the next day. Maybe he can complete a few chores for her, clean up, iron, wash the dishes, or make her something to eat. As long as he's putting aside time to serve her while she views her show, he will be joining her at some level.

He should also make sure that he asks his wife positive questions about the show afterwards, so that he can connect with her. Questions like, "How was the show?" and "What happened this week?" not only help the husband in joining his wife, but also help him to discern how she's being spiritually impacted by that particular program.

If a man's wife watches something on television that he dislikes, but "does not" feel compromises his spiritual development, he should make every attempt to watch that program with her. By nature, we form connectors with things and people that resonate with us. As a result, whatever (and whomever) we connect with gains access to our heart. It's therefore important that a man understand the things his wife connects with, how he himself can connect with those things. If a man's wife connects with a show that he has no interest in, he shouldn't leave her alone to watch that program. He should try watching that program with her, and at the very least find out why she's captivated by it. A husband must demonstrate interest in those things his wife is captivated by.

Think about those 86,400 seconds that you get in a single

day. Are you managing those seconds in ways that bring you closer to your wife?

(#6) AREA OF JOINING: FINANCES

The sixth area that a husband must join his wife is the area of finances. Probably no other area digs up as much uneasiness in relationships as the subject of money. There's something about money that always ends up pulling out the worst in people. The lack of it (or loss of it) creates tension inside of us, and threatens even the closest of relationships.

Money represents many different things to many different people. For some, money is simply a means to an end. For others, money is the complete embodiment of power, authority, independence and self-worth all rolled into one. Because money has so many deep connections to the human psyche, it often serves as one of the greatest motivators of human wrongdoing.

In Mark 10:25, a young rich man approaches Jesus to find out how he can obtain eternal life. After a series of exchanges between the two, Jesus zeroes in on the young man's attachment to money. "If you want to be perfect, go, sell your possessions and give to the poor, and you will have treasure in heaven. Then come, follow me," Jesus said. When the young man heard these words, he was crushed. He was crushed because he knew that he couldn't bring himself to do what Jesus asked of him. He couldn't give up the very thing that he was attached to. He couldn't give up the security, comfort, and overall gratification that came to him by virtue of his wealth.

In Chapter 5 (Marriage Principle #3) we said that husbands and wives must not build their marriage from a place of separation, but rather they must build their marriage from a place of oneness. "She has her money, I have mine." "She has her bills, I have mine." She has her investments, I have mine." Many couples want to live "separate and distinct" lives financially, but at the same time want "an abundance of unity" in every other aspect of their marriage. That's like going out and bar-hopping every night, but desiring more quality time at home with your wife. The way of life contradicts the desired result.

When married couples operate "as separate individuals" in the area of finances, the natural result will be "separation" in the area of finances. It's that simple. Things like separate bank accounts, separate name use (maiden name use), separate living arrangements, and separation agreements (prenuptial agreements), all subtly build separation into the life of a marriage.

Some men may ask the question, "If a husband and wife have two separate bank accounts, is their marriage doomed?" Well, the issue is not whether or not the marriage is doomed; the issue is what type of seed is sown into the marriage through their actions. In other words, do the separate bank accounts sow a seed of unity into the relationship, or do they sow a seed of separation? The word "joint" denotes unity, so I would definitely say that a "joint bank" account sows a seed of unity within the marriage (especially when the management of that account is balanced and equitable). On the flip side, the word "separate" denotes separation, so I would say that a "separate bank account" sows a seed of separation within a marriage. The moment you give birth to anything "separate" within a relationship you've instantly sown a seed of separation into it. It does not mean the marriage is doomed, it just means that separation has been sown into the relationship.

I know several couples that maintain both separate and joint banking accounts. Many of these relationships appear to be solid even as they enjoy the benefits of these accounts. I won't argue the fact that there are benefits to having separate checking accounts. But at the same time, we cannot forget that there's only two types of seed that can be sown into a marriage; a seed of oneness or a seed of separation. The more challenges that a couple has in the area of oneness, the more likely it is that they are sowing seeds of separation into their relationship. If a husband wants to sow a seed of unity into his relationship, joining in the area of finances is a great place to start.

In Ezekiel 37, God told the prophet, "JOIN the two sticks together so that they could become one in my hand." In Matthew 19, Jesus said "for this reason a man must JOIN to his wife, and the two will become one flesh." Time and time again God shows us that unity precedes oneness. And so it is, that in order for the husband and wife to successfully "become one," they must be joined in the life they live together.

Chapter 7

A Husband's Vision

The Husband Must Watch Over His Family

"Son of man, I have made you a watchman for the people of
Israel"

Ezekiel 3:16

"The Husband as Head"

When God deputized the husband to assume the position of
"head" within the marriage union (Ephesians 5:23), this was in
all likelihood, one of God's most important assignments. It was
more important than the assignment of Priests, Prophets, and
Kings in the Old Testament. It was even more important than
the assignment of Apostles, Evangelists, and Teachers in the
New Testament. No other assignment rivals that of the
husband's assignment, because it's the one assignment that
Jesus fulfilled himself, as husband to a body of believers called,
"the Church."

The Husband's position as "head" is an extremely important
one. But as important as this position is, we must be mindful

that his position is just that; a position. It does not speak to the husband's capabilities in occupying that position; nor does it speak to the husband's present level of competence or commitment towards fulfilling the position. A husband could be absolutely incompetent, dysfunctional and uncommitted, and yet still qualify to occupy the position of "head" within his marriage. Headship is not aptitude-based position. It's a position that the husband owns simply because God gave it to him.

When God gave the husband the position of "head" within the marriage union, it certainly wasn't meant to be an indictment on the wife. In other words, God didn't give him the position because he felt the husband knew more than his wife. And it wasn't because the husband was better than his wife in God's sight. So why did God make the husband "The Head?" The position was assigned simply because God needed someone within the family unit who would lay their life down so that all of its members could live. He wanted someone to own the role of "burden bearer," "sacrificial lamb," and "wounded-healer." God gave the husband the position of headship because he wanted someone who would be able to live and lead like Him. This would not be an easy task for the husband to fulfill, especially when the example for the position is the ultimate husband, Jesus Christ.

"The Watchman"

The husband was not given his position because of his aptitude, but there are some skill sets that can help the husband in becoming more apt at handling his position. Probably the most significant of all skill sets that a husband can adopt is the skill of vision.

Some men run away from vision like the plague, and say, "I don't want it, let my wife handle it." Other men grab the visionary role and become so zealous with it that they end up operating like quasi-dictators within the home. Regardless of which posture the husband takes, **he must understand that the visionary position is not about governance, it's about leadership**. And in order for a husband to lead his wife and children, he must become a "watchman." That meaning, he must have a vision, and the ability to guide his family according to that vision. The watchman is the eyes for those that he watches over. He is their protector and overseer. God has made the husband a watchman over his wife and family.

"Sight, Insight and Foresight"

The watchman operates utilizing three distinct levels of

vision: Sight, Insight, and Foresight. *Sight* is the ability to see those things that are readily in front of you. *Insight* is the ability to see those things that are beyond what is readily in front of you. *Foresight* is the ability to see those things that are yet to come before you. These three levels of vision help the husband form a comprehensive understanding of his family's needs, as he empowers them to become all that they can in Christ. Sight, Insight, and Foresight play a significant role in the husband's ability to successfully lead his family. The remainder of this chapter will highlight these three areas, as well as offer guidance on how the godly husband applies these things within his daily walk.

"Sight"

Sight allows a husband's to see those things that are readily before him. Jesus refers to it as "a blessing." In Matthew 13 Jesus tells his disciples, "blessed are your eyes because they see, and your ears because they hear. For truly I tell you, many prophets and righteous people longed to see what you see but did not see it, and to hear what you hear but did not hear it" (Matthew 13:16-17). Jesus makes the point to His disciples that they were blessed to be able to see and observe Him with their very own eyes. The apostle John also captured it in the book of John when he said, "That which was from the beginning, which we have heard, which we have seen with our eyes, which we have looked at and our hands have touched— this we proclaim concerning the Word of life" (1 John 1:1). Sight wasn't just meant to be a blessing for those who saw Jesus in person. Sight was meant to be a blessing to all who would have the opportunity to see Jesus in their day-to-day lives. As husbands, we are blessed to be able to see Christ through our wives each and every day. We are blessed to be able to see Christ through our children each and every day. We are blessed to be able to see Christ through our loved ones and our family members each and every day.

According to the bible, **sight isn't just a blessing; sight is a responsibility**. We aren't just blessed to see, we actually have a responsibility to see. God gives us the blessing of sight so that we can respond to the needs of others. Whenever we see a need that exists in another person's life, we have the responsibility to try and meet that need to the best of our ability (whether through prayer, words of encouragement, money, or a kind gesture). How many times have you seen someone upset about something, but didn't stop to comfort them? How many times have you seen someone frustrated about something, but yet you continued to ignore them? How many times have you seen someone struggling with bags, but yet you didn't lend a hand to help them? God gives us the blessing of sight, not just for our own exclusive use, but for the people who need it the most. God doesn't want us to walk away from those in need. He doesn't want us to become judgmental or critical towards these individuals. God wants us to take the blessing of sight and use it to help others. If a godly husband sees someone who is hungry, his automatic response should be, "Can I get you a meal?" If a godly husband sees someone who is sad, his automatic response should be, "Is there anything I can do for you?" If a godly husband sees someone who is worried he should say, "Don't worry, you're going to make it through this." This is how a godly husband converts his sight into a tangible commodity that others can benefit from.

Sight is not just his blessing, sight is his responsibility. In Matthew 25 Jesus made it clear to the unrighteous that their sight wasn't just their blessing, it was their responsibility as well. It was their responsibility in that, they had an obligation to respond to those that they saw in need. Having the ability to see is a blessing. But with that blessing comes a responsibility to respond to those things that you see.

What if a man sees his wife spiritually hungry, thirsty, unclothed, or in prison? What type of responsibility does God place upon the husband in this situation? We already know from Matthew 25 that if a husband fails to visit a stranger in prison, he fails to visit Jesus in prison. So how much more severe is the offense in God's eyes if a husband fails to visit his wife in prison? I Timothy chapter 5:8 captures the essence of how God feels about this matter. It simply reads, "If anyone does not provide for his relatives, and especially for his immediate family, he has denied the faith and is worse than an unbeliever." In essence, when a husband ignores the needs of his wife; when he chooses not to offer her a drink from the well of salvation; when he refuses to warm her with the clothing of Christ; he's actually considered "worse than an unbeliever."

Blessed are the husband's eyes, for they are able to see his wife. And his sight is not just his blessing; it's his responsibility. **As a watchman, the husband has a responsibility to see his wife, and respond to the things that impact her world. He's responsible for intuitively identifying her areas of need and concern.** This actually sounds like a high level of responsibility for the husband, but really it's not. We actually have domestic relations laws in the United States that require a husband to help his wife **if he sees her** in imminent danger. Simply put, if a husband sees his wife in imminent danger, but chooses to ignore her, or fails to get help for her in a timely manner, he could be held liable in a court of law. Not only that, but there are laws in the United States that actually hold a husband responsible for what he "did not see but should have seen" in his marriage. If the laws of the United States hold such a high regard for spousal accountability, shouldn't the godly husband's regard be that much greater?

"Insight"

In the last section, we defined sight as "a husband's ability to see those things that are readily in front of him." We said that sight gives a husband the opportunity to draw certain conclusions about things and people based on external observations. That's sight in a nutshell. Insight, on the other hand, goes beyond external observation into the world that lies beneath. Insight is **"a husband's ability to see those things that are beyond what's readily in front of him."** This takes sight to the next level by moving it from a behavioral conversation to a motivational conversation. A sight study says "I see the behavior and I don't like it." An insight study says "I see the behavior and I don't like it, but I know that there's something beyond what I see that's motivating this person to behave this way." Insight causes a man to look beyond the obvious and explore the spiritual, psychological and emotional motivations behind a person's behavior. Insight doesn't excuse the way a person behaves; it simply gives a snapshot into the world in which they live.

In Matthew 16:2-4 Jesus told the Pharisees, "You know how to interpret the appearance of the sky, but you cannot interpret the sign of the times." Jesus indicts the Pharasees for putting all their energy and effort into studying and interpreting the patterns of weather and season, while overlooking the patterns of biblical prophecy that were now coming to fruition in front of their very own eyes. Jesus was essentially saying that if they just took a moment to look beyond the external, they could discover who He really was. This is the essence of insight.

As a watchman, it's the husband's job to see beyond the surface and delve into the internal world that his wife and children live in. There's no doubt that a man's wife and children have an internal world that they inhabit. But seldom does the husband tap into those worlds. Some husbands are just altogether unaware of these things; other husbands may be aware, but are just too scared to explore such rough terrains. Regardless of which category a man falls into, one thing is for certain; **problems arise when a man fails to interpret "the signs of the times" within the lives of people**. Problems arise when a man fails to exercise "insight."

Proverbs 16:21 refers to the wise in heart as "discerning." A discerning man looks beyond the external in order to uncover the truth about a given thing. When a man exercises this level of wisdom, he exercises insight. A sight-driven person says, "What do I see when I look at my wife?" An insight-driven person says "What's behind what I see when I look at my wife?" Sight says "What's going on with my wife's behavior?" Insight says, "What's going on with my wife's heart?" This is godly wisdom at its finest.

For the man of insight, it takes work; hard work. It takes

hard work for him to dig deep and discover what's truly going on within his wife's heart. It takes hard work for him to sort through the depths of his wife's pains and frustrations. It takes hard work for him to look beyond his wife's external faults so that he can satisfy her internal needs. It takes work to do all of these things. But the man of insight is equipped for the job.

Paul shared a prayer with the Philippians that really opened up my perspective on the subject of insight. He said to them, "This is my prayer: that your love may abound more and more in knowledge and depth of insight" (Philippians 1:9). In effect, Paul's prayer was that the Philippians grew in love. And the path to growing in love would come through growing in the area of insight. Paul was saying that the more insight they established, the greater their ability to love. And I would have to say that as a husband, this principle has absolutely held true. The more insight that I've gained into my wife, the more effective I have been in my ability to love her and meet her needs. A husband's insight cannot remain stagnant; but rather, it must be dynamic, progressive and ever-changing, even as his wife grows and changes.

"Foresight"

The last and most vital component of vision is "foresight."

163

Foresight is "a husband's ability to see those things that are yet to come before him." Foresight is different from sight and insight, in that sight and insight examine things that exist, while foresight examines things that don't exist, but will exist in the future. Foresight is about having sight and insight before the need for sight and insight arises.

A husband will encounter many challenges within his marriage that he'll need to recognize well before they actually occur. Let's take arguments for example. If a husband consistently studies his wife and works hard at interpreting the world that she lives, he puts himself in a great position to foresee an argument with her way before it manifests. And when a man is really proficient at this, he can walk around his home and immediately identify those things that will likely cause strife between him and his wife.

"A Husband Must Foresee Offenses Against Him"

A husband also has the ability to use foresight in order to anticipate potential offenses against him. For example, if his wife offends him on a consistent basis, he might use foresight to help him anticipate her next offense in advance. All conflict comes from within (James 4:1), so if a man's wife exhibits behavior that repeatedly ushers him into conflict with her, that man must first look at himself in order to better understand the source of his vulnerabilities. Foresight gives a husband the opportunity to think about those vulnerabilities in advance, so that he can be prepared with Christ-like responses when these offenses arrive at his door-step.

Foresight isn't just about "seeing in advance," it's about what the husband does with what he sees. If every year my wife forgets my birthday, I must come to terms with the fact that at least once a year this offense is coming. I know it's coming, (because every year I have a birthday) but now I have to prepare myself for how I am going to respond when she forgets. Am I going to be crushed every year she forgets my birthday? Am I going to argue with her when it happens yet again? Am I going to feel that I'm worth nothing to her because she forgets my birthday every year? It's not enough for me to just know the offense is coming. I have to plan for how I'm going to spiritually and emotionally deal with the offense when it comes. And trust me; the chances are high that this offense will occur over and over again.

Think about mood swings. All of us have mood swings. Mood swings are called "swings" because of their sporadic nature. Sometimes our wives are up, and sometimes they are down (the same thing applies for husbands). Mood swings are not a surprise; yet, when a mood swing comes, we're somehow shocked and offended by its existence. We put all our energy into cursing our wife's mood. But the reality is, our wife's behavior (while frustrating) isn't anything out of the norm. They behave the same way over and over again each month around that time, and we become frustrated over and over again. It's a pattern that the husband has the ability to break simply by exercising foresight. As husbands, we must ask ourselves, "When I see my wife in a mood swing, do I remain calm and take note of her pattern? Do I use my understanding of her mood to help reduce her stress and limit my chances of conflict with her? Do I find ways to help make her a better, stronger woman in spite of her mood? The answers to these questions will reveal just how prevalent foresight is within your marriage.

The Husband Must Foresee His Offenses Against Others

A husband uses foresight to not only anticipate his wife's potential offenses against him, but he also uses foresight to anticipate his potential offenses against his wife. Most husbands have at least one habit, or pattern of behavior that in some way irritates their wife. It's a husband's job to understand these behaviors and do what he can to avoid them. That doesn't mean that a husband has to "walk on eggshells" with his wife. It doesn't mean that he avoids discussing difficult issues with her. **It simply means that he carefully examines the risks that he assumes by doing things that repeatedly offend his wife.** A husband must foresee the manifestation of these offenses, and do what is necessary to prevent them from occurring.

A man without foresight will find himself saying and doing things that distance himself from his wife, without realizing why. Some men are in the habit of casually uttering belittling remarks about their wife's weight, age, physical appearance, cooking, family etc. They share these sentiments without understanding the emotional hemorrhaging induced through their criticism. Because of desensitization, that man cannot foresee the pending destruction that awaits his marriage as a result of his words.

A Man Foresees Potentially Divisive Influences

A husband doesn't only exercise foresight in his relationship with his wife; he exercises foresight in every other relationship that exists in his life. We know that as a risk manager, the husband is tasked with protecting the marriage asset from potentially divisive influences. Foresight helps a husband in doing just that. Foresight causes a husband to reassess the time that he spends talking to that female friend at work who always wants to have lunch with him. Foresight causes a husband to avoid certain "links" that he encounters while surfing on the internet. Foresight causes a husband to be selective with whom he befriends and interacts with on Facebook. A husband uses foresight to identify those people, places, and things in his life that can potentially become a divisive influence within his marriage.

A man's obsession with things gadgets, technology, social media, and sports can potentially compromise his ability to exercise foresight. For example, if a married man stays in front of the television all day Sunday watching football and goes to bed after midnight (when the games end), that man has let self-gratification override foresight. If a man is constantly on his IPAD or IPHONE, or immerses himself in Facebook and Twitter all day, that man has let self-gratification override foresight. In all likelihood, these decisions will at some point become the source of arguments between him and his wife. Foresight helps a man see these arguments before they manifest, so that he can make the necessary changes in his decision-making.

A Husband's Vision: Conclusion

The most important thing for the godly husband to understand about vision is that it originates from the heart. That means, the essential elements of vision (sight, insight and foresight) only work to the degree that our hearts remain fully healthy and submitted to the Lord. If a man's heart is wounded, jaded, or hardened, his vision will be greatly impaired. A man's vision quality is a product of the light that dwells within his heart. In Matthew 6:22 Jesus said, "The eye is the lamp of the body. If your eyes are good, your whole body will be full of light. If your eyes are bad, your whole body will be filled with darkness." Thus, the condition of a man's heart gives rise to his vision, and his vision impacts the state of his entire body. Titus 1:15 says "To the pure, all things are pure, but to those who are corrupted and do not believe, nothing is pure. In fact, both their minds and consciences are corrupted." So if the watchman functions with a jaded heart, everything that he looks at will be jaded; which will inevitably contaminate his entire body. But if on the other hand the watchman's heart is pure, he'll see life and people through the lens of purity; which then purifies his entire body.

The watchman must understand that his heart fuels the

vision that he has for himself, his wife, and his family; and plays a central role in the exercising of sight, insight and foresight. A man's heart is the vehicle by which he uncovers the truth about people, circumstances, and situations. His heart prevents him from making decisions that threaten the life of his marriage asset. The watchman must protect his heart at all times in order to protect the destiny of his household.

Chapter 8

A Husband's Scriptures

A Husband's 24 Greatest Discoveries

(1)
The Father's Exclusivity - *Isaiah 43:11*
"I, even I, am the LORD, and apart from me there is no savior."

(2)
The Son's Exclusivity - *Acts 4:12*
"Salvation is found in no one else, for there is no other name under heaven given to mankind by which we must be saved."

(3)
The Father's Preeminence - *Exodus 34:14*
"Do not worship any other god, for the LORD, whose name is Jealous, is a jealous God."

(4)
The Son's Preeminence - *John 6:35*
"Then Jesus declared, "I am the Bread of life. Whoever comes to me will never go hungry, and whoever believes in me will never be thirsty."

(5)
The Father's Creation - *Isaiah 44:24*
"I am the LORD, the Maker of all things, who stretches out the heavens, who spreads out the earth by myself..."

(6)
The Son's Creation - *John 1:10*
"He was in the world, and though the world was made through him, the world did not recognize him."

(7)
The Husband's Need for a Savior - *I Timothy 1:15*

"Christ Jesus came into the world to save sinners—of whom I am the worst.

(8)
God's Love for The Husband - *John 3:16*

"For God so loved the world, that he gave his one and only Son, that whoever believes in him shall not perish but have eternal life."

(9)
The Husband's Path to Salvation - *Romans 10:9*

"If you declare with your mouth, 'Jesus is Lord,' and believe in your heart that God raised him from the dead, you will be saved."

(10)
The Husband's Identity - *2 Corinthians 5:17*

"Therefore, if anyone is in Christ, the new creation has come: The old has gone, the new is here!"

(11)
The Husband's Character - *1 Samuel 10:6*

"The Spirit of the LORD will come powerfully upon you, and you will prophesy with them; and you will be changed into a different person."

(12)
The Husband's Strength - *Acts 1:8*

"But you will receive power when the Holy spirit comes on you.."

(13)
The Husband's Transformation - *Romans 12:2*

"Do not conform to the pattern of this world, but be transformed by the renewing of your mind."

(14)
The Husband's First Ministry - *2 Corinthians 5:18*

"All this is from God, who reconciled us to himself through Christ and gave us the ministry of reconciliation: that God was reconciling the world to himself in Christ, not counting people's sins against them."

(15)
The Husband's Biggest Struggle - *Galatians 5:17*
"For the flesh desires what is contrary to the Spirit, and the Spirit what is contrary to the flesh. They are in conflict with each other, so that you are not to do whatever you want.."

(16)
The Husband's Greatest Responsibility - *Matthew 22:37-38*
"Jesus replied: 'Love the Lord your God with all your heart and with all your soul and with all your mind.' This is the first and greatest commandment."

(17)
The Husband's Second Greatest Responsibility - *Matt 22:39-40*
"And the second is like it: 'Love your neighbor as yourself.' All the Law and the Prophets hang on these two commandments."

(18)
The Husband's Covenant Responsibility - *Mark 10:7-9*
"For this reason a man will leave his father and mother and be united to his wife, and the two will become one flesh. So they are no longer two, but one flesh. Therefore what God has joined together, let no one separate."

(19)
The Husband's Love For His Wife - *Ephesians 5:25-27*
"Husbands, love your wives, just as Christ loved the church and gave himself up for her to make her holy, cleansing her by the washing with water through the word, and to present her to himself as a radiant church, without stain or wrinkle or any other blemish, but holy and blameless."

(20)
The Husband's Management Of His Family - *I Timothy 3:4-5*
"He must manage his own family well and see that his children obey him, and he must do so in a manner worthy of full respect. (If anyone does not know how to manage his own family, how can he take care of God's church?)"

(21)

The Husband's Servanthood Unto His Family - *Luke 22:26 (NASB)*

"But *it is* not this way with you, but the one who is the greatest among you must become like the youngest, and the leader like the servant."

(22)

The Husband's Provision For His Family - *I Timothy 5:8*

"But if anyone does not provide for his own, and especially for those of his household, he has denied the faith and is worse than an unbeliever."

(23)

The Husband's Care For His Family – *Ezekiel 34:2*

"This is what the Sovereign LORD says: Woe to you shepherds of Israel who only take care of yourselves! Should not shepherds take care of the flock? You eat the curds, clothe yourselves with the wool and slaughter the choice animals, but you do not take care of the flock."

(24)

The Husband's Lifeline - *Deuteronomy 32:46-47*

"Take to heart all the words I have solemnly declared to you this day... They are not just idle words for you – they are your life."

Chapter 9

A Husband's Devotional

Meditations and Insights for a Godly Husband

➤ **THE SPIRIT OF THE LORD CHANGES THE HUSBAND INTO A DIFFERENT PERSON.**

"The Spirit of the LORD will come upon you in power, and you will prophesy with them; and you will be changed into a different person." (1 Samuel 10:6)

➤ **A HUSBAND'S SALVATION MUST PRODUCE FRUIT.**

"May you always be filled with the fruit of your salvation - the righteous character produced in your life by Jesus Christ - for this will bring much glory and praise to God." (Philippians 1:11 – NLT)

➤ **A HUSBAND'S GREATEST DESIRE MUST BE FOR THE LORD.**

"Whom have I in heaven but you? And earth has nothing I desire besides you." (Psalms 73:25)

➤ **IT'S A HUSBAND'S PRIVILEGE TO SUFFER FOR CHRIST.**

"For you have been given not only the privilege of trusting in Christ but also the privilege of suffering for him." (Philippians 1:29 - NLT)

Godly Husband's Notes on Philippians 1:29 - We tend to use the word "suffering" much too casually within our relationships. Often we will utter the words, "I'm suffering within this marriage" "I'm suffering with the way I'm being treated." "She's making me suffer through this separation." Often times these are not true examples of suffering. In fact, many of us will live and die never knowing what it truly means to suffer. But be that as it may, we cannot overlook the fact that there are in fact some situations where people are truly suffering within their marriage. And in those situations, we must ask ourselves two essential questions: (1) Has God called them to endure suffering in that particular situation? If so, (2) are they willing to endure the suffering that God has called them to?

Without hesitation, most people would answer a resounding "no" to both of these questions if ever asked. But when we think about it, why wouldn't God allow our suffering? By allowing us to suffer, does it diminish God's love for us in any way? Or maybe the better question is, "did God's love for His Son diminish when he allowed Him to suffer?" Absolutely not. In fact God's love for His Son was even more profound because of his willingness to humbly suffer, and die as an innocent man. God knew that behind his Son's suffering was a greater purpose; and that purpose was life for all mankind. So why would he not deem us worthy to suffer for a great cause? What if God came to you and told you that all cancer would be eradicated if you simply endured suffering for one entire year. Would you be willing to suffer so that millions of lives could be saved? If your answer is yes, to what degree of suffering would you be willing to endure? Jesus carried his obedience past the point of suffering all the way to his death. As a husband, how far would you be willing to carry your obedience? If God asked you to endure 5 years of suffering within your marriage so that you could enjoy 50 years of marital prosperity, would you do it?

➢ A HUSBAND'S HUMILITY PAVES THE WAY FOR HIS DEATH.

"After he had appeared in human form, he abased and humbled himself (still further) and carried obedience to the extreme of death, even the death of the cross. (Philippians 2:8 – AMP)

Godly Husband's Notes on Philippians 2:8: - In our previous paragraph we asked the question "How far will you carry your obedience to God?" Jesus clearly sets the bar by carrying his obedience to the point of death. But what does death look like for the husband at a practical level? Maybe it's him remaining faithful in a marriage where his wife remains unfaithful. Maybe it's him being honest his business dealings even though it hurts him financially. Maybe it's him giving away most of his paycheck to someone without receiving any recognition or reward. Maybe it's him serving someone that doesn't respect him. To what extent will a husband carry out his obedience to God within his marriage?

➢ GOD ADMIRES THE HUSBAND WHO IS HUMBLE.

"This is the one I esteem: he who is humble and contrite in spirit, and trembles at my word." (Isaiah 66:2)

➢ A HUSBAND'S POSITION IN THE KINGDOM OF HEAVEN IS DETERMINED BY HIS LEVEL OF HUMILITY.

"So anyone who becomes as humble as this little child is the greatest in the Kingdom of Heaven." (Matthew 18:4)

➢ A HUSBAND MUST IDENTIFY HIS SOURCE OF HEALING.

"...if my people, who are called by my name, will humble themselves and pray and seek my face and turn from their wicked ways, then will I hear from heaven and will forgive their sin and will heal their land." (1 Chronicles 7:14)

➢ A HUSBAND MUST WHOLEHEARTEDLY SEEK THE LORD.

"My soul is consumed with longing for your laws at all times." (Psalm 11:20)

➢ THE HUSBAND'S HERITAGE IS IN THE WORD OF GOD.

"Your statutes are my heritage forever" (Psalm 119:111)

➢ THE HUSBAND MUST STRIVE FOR A BLAMELESS LIFE.

"I will be careful to lead a blameless life." (Psalm 101:2)

Godly Husband's Notes on Psalm 101:2 - Jesus is the only person ever to live a completely blameless life. That means the only way a man can achieve a blameless life is by inviting "the one who is blameless" into his heart. Psalm 101 highlights nine traits that demonstrate a "blameless life." Those nine traits are specifically listed out in the next chapter, along with accompanying scriptures. Take a look at these nine traits and figure out which areas you could improve in, and how you'll go about making those improvements.

➢ A HUSBAND MUST KNOW WHAT'S CONTROLLING HIM.

"For when we were controlled by the sinful nature, the sinful passions aroused by the law were at work in our bodies, so that we bore fruit for death." (Romans 7:5)

Godly Husband's Notes on Romans 7:5 - At any given point in time, a godly husband may find himself under the control sinful desires. If he doesn't consistently monitor the things that influence him, he'll find himself ripe for deception and destruction.

More Godly Husband's Notes on Romans 7:5 - When a godly husband sees something that's enticing to him, the first thing he should do is wait. Why should he wait? He waits because he realizes that sinful desires have the ability to mute the voice of God in his life. And without the voice of God, he's at the mercy of his own sensual desires and inclinations. This puts him in an extremely vulnerable position. So the best thing for the husband to do (at times) is wait before pursuing something that he's attracted to. When a man delays his indulgences, he gives himself the spiritual spacing necessary to figure out where his enticements originate. That enables him to rightly judge the authenticity of his desires, and positions his heart to hear clearly from the Lord.

More Godly Husband's Notes on Romans 7:5- The godly husband must realize that he will often be controlled by self-interests. Just ask Abraham, who essentially handed his wife Sarah over to Pharaoh in order to save himself. Or Isaac, who did the same exact thing with his wife Rebecca. You can even ask Saul, who tried to kill his mentee David in order to save his own image. When the godly husband becomes controlled by self-interests, he puts himself and others around him in an extremely dangerous position.

More Godly Husband's Notes on Romans 7:5 - As a godly husband, do you know how to distinguish your own desires from the desires of God? Can you tell when your desires are running contrary to His? If you already know how to figure this out, I applaud you. But if you struggle with this (as many of us do), please know that God offers us wonderful tools to help us sort through this process. Prayer, worship, fasting, study of The Word, and godly counsel all act as "sifters" to help us separate our own personal views from God's views.

Knowing the will of God can be one of the easiest, yet most complex undertakings in the husband's life. Sinful desires can sometimes be so strong that they literally override the voice of God inside the husband. Knowing this, I recommend that the godly husband always do the math. Even though he knows that $2 + 2 = 4$, he should still write it out. Why? So that he can see each number's individual value, and understand how each number relates to the other. When the godly husband is confronted with a decision, he shouldn't immediately rush into it. He should first make sure that the voice he is following is the Lord's voice and not his flesh. He should make sure that nothing else is controlling him or his decision. He should use prayer, study, worship, fasting, and godly counsel to help him distinguish his views from the Lord's views. He must sit down and do the math.

➤ A HUSBAND'S LIFESTYLE PERMEATES HIS MINDSET.

"Those who live according to the sinful nature have their minds set on what that nature desires; but those who live in accordance with the Spirit have their minds set on what the Spirit desires." (Romans 8:5)

➤ THERE'S ONLY ONE "TRUE" VINE FOR THE HUSBAND.

"I am the true vine, and my father is the gardener. "
(John 15:1 - NLT)

Godly Husband's Notes on John 15:1 - A husband may have many different types of vines that he attaches himself to over the course of his life (i.e. relationships, finances, work, education, religion etc.) But Jesus refers to himself as the "true vine." That means that Jesus is the only vine through which the husband can produce Kingdom Fruit. The godly husband may experience many different levels of productivity over the course of his life. But his greatest and most authentic form of productivity comes when he attaches himself to the "True Vine."

➤ A HUSBAND HAS NOTHING EXCEPT FOR WHAT GOD GIVES HIM.

"A man can receive nothing [he can claim nothing, he can take unto himself nothing] except as it has been granted to him from heaven." (John 3:27 - AMP)

➤ A HUSBAND MUST ACCEPT DECREASE IN ORDER TO PRODUCE INCREASE.

"He must become greater and greater, and I must become less and less." (John 3:30 –NLT)

Godly Husband's Notes on John 3:30 - Whatever issues that a husband has in his life, his solution will always be, "He must become greater, and I must become lesser." That will solve any and all the husband's problems 100% of the time, guaranteed. More of Christ, less of himself.

➤ GOD WANTS THE HUSBAND TO PRAISE HIM AFTER HE'S BEEN SATISFIED.

"I am sending you grain, new wine and oil, enough to satisfy you fully; never again will I make you an object of scorn to the nations. You will have plenty to eat, until you are full, and you will praise the name of the LORD your God, who has worked wonders for you..." (Joel 2:19)

The Godly Husband's Notes on Joel 2:19 - A man will always maintain a certain level of respect and appreciation for those things (and people) which satisfy him. Thus, it's not uncommon for a man to show respect and appreciation for God by praying before he eats a meal. He is thankful that God has fulfilled a particular need in his life, so he expresses that appreciation by praying before he eats. But what does he do "after" he has eaten his meal and has been satisfied? What does he do after he's received his much anticipated gratification? Does he pray yet again? Does he thank God with the same level of thanksgiving and appreciation that he did when he was hungry?

Many men praise God before they eat, but not as many will praise Him afterwards. God desires that the husband not only praise him before he is filled, but after as well. In Hosea 13:6 the Lord says this concerning the people of Israel: "When I fed them they were satisfied; when they were satisfied, they became proud; then they forgot me." This is how a people forgets their humble beginnings.

Before a man is fed, he is hungry; and in his hunger he seeks both fulfillment and satisfaction. But after he is fed and is satisfied, pride seeps into his heart. This leads him to a place of forgetfulness. I can think of many times when this has happened to me. I wanted something so bad, and after finally getting it I forgot how hungry I was when I initially desired it. The key to the godly husband's gratefulness and appreciation for God is praise before and after he is satisfied.

➢ GOD WANTS TO REVEAL HIMSELF TO THOSE CLOSEST TO THE HUSBAND.

"The people you live among will see how awesome is the work that I the Lord will do for you." (Exodus 34:10)

Godly Husband's Notes on Exodus 34:10: Ultimately, God

wants to impact the life of those who are closest to the husband; including his wife, his children, his parents, his friends, his family, his co-workers and anyone else that is close to him. God desires to reach the world through the husband. If the husband for some reason fails to exemplify Christ within his daily walk, he misses a golden opportunity to transform the lives of those closest to him.

> ## A HUSBAND MUST KEEP HIS WORD EVEN WHEN IT HURTS, BUT NEVER WHEN IT'S WRONG.

"LORD, who may dwell in your sanctuary? Who may live on your holy hill? He whose walk is blameless and who does what is righteous, who speaks the truth from his heart and has no slander on his tongue, who does his neighbor no wrong and casts no slur on his fellowman, who despises a vile man but honors those who fear the LORD, _who keeps his oath even when it hurts_, who lends his money without usury and does not accept a bribe against the innocent. He who does these things will never be shaken." (Psalm 15:1-5)

Godly Husband's Notes on Psalm 15:1-5 - One of the godly husband's greatest struggles is becoming consistent in his ability to keep his word. There are many people in the godly husband's life that place demands upon him (i.e. his wife, his children, his family, his community, his employer, his creditors, etc.). And because he desperately wants to honor all of these competing demands, he ends up making commitments that he's incapable of fulfilling. So like a bank account without funds, the godly husband's commitments get bounced because he just doesn't have enough in his account to pay off his debt. And when a man breaks promises over and over again, his credibility and trustworthiness diminish.

Psalm 15:4 reminds us that a man's ability to keep his word is one of the defining aspects of his relationship with the Lord. When a man keeps his word (even to the point of his own detriment) he demonstrates the fact that his commitment wasn't made unto men, but unto God.

More Godly Husband's Notes on Psalm 15:1-5 - There will be times when a husband makes commitments that God does not approve of. In these situations, it's never wrong for the husband to rethink or retract a commitment. He may have made the commitment on impulse; or maybe he tried to think it through, but sinful desires took root and clouded his judgment. Regardless of how the husband arrived at his bad choice, he must have the courage to reverse that choice if it hinders his relationship with God. Every single commitment that a man makes must be judged by how it impacts his relationship with God.

The one commitment that a godly husband must not retract is the marriage commitment (also known as the "marriage covenant"). If a man makes a commitment to the covenant of marriage, but later decides that his commitment was made in error, he mustn't abandon that commitment. He must honor the commitment he has made before God and his wife.

More Godly Husband's Notes on Psalm 15:1-5 - The marriage covenant is different than any other type of commitment, in that it creates a lifetime bond between a man, a woman and God. This three party covenant stays intact for as long as two of the three participants remains faithful to it. So if God and the husband both remain faithful to the marriage covenant, it will remain intact despite the wife's unfaithfulness to it. Similarly, if God and the wife both remain faithful to the marriage covenant, it will remain intact despite the husband's unfaithfulness to it. God himself will always remain faithful to the marriage covenant regardless of the husband's or wife's level of commitment. His faithfulness to the covenant never changes.

> ## A HUSBAND'S SUCCESS IS NOT DETERMINED BY HIS ABILITY TO ASK, BUT HIS ABILITY TO "KEEP" ASKING.

"Keep on asking and it will be given you; keep on seeking and you will find; keep on knocking [reverently] and [the door] will be opened to you." (Matthew 7:7 – AMP)

Godly Husband's Notes on Matthew 7:7 - It takes a special kind of husband to have the guts to knock. But it takes an exceptional kind of husband to have the guts to "KEEP" knocking.

> ## A HUSBAND'S BATTLES DO NOT BELONG TO HIM.

"One man of you shall put to flight a thousand, for it is the Lord your God who fights for you, as he promised you." (Joshua 23:10 – AMP)

Godly Husband's Notes on Joshua 23:10 - It's great to know that God has jurisdiction over the husband's battles. But it's equally important to know that even as God fights his battles, he still must guard himself. And by "guarding" I don't mean in the physical sense. I'm referring to the guarding of the heart. Don't get me wrong, there's nothing wrong with locking your car door, looking both ways before you cross the street, or even buying life insurance. These types of things guard the husband in the physical sense. However, none of these things are able to guard the husband against a spiritual attack. The guarding of the heart is one of the few things that can accomplish this.

➤ WHEN A HUSBAND FEELS LIKE HIS LIFE IS SLIPPING AWAY, LET HIM REMEMBER THE LORD.

"As my life was slipping away, I remembered the Lord. And my earnest prayer went out to you in your holy Temple." (Jonah 2:7 – NLT)

➤ GOD REQUIRES THE HUSBAND TO PAY CLOSE ATTENTION.

"Which of you will listen to this or pay close attention in time to come?" (Isaiah 42:23)

➤ THE HUSBAND SHOULD KEEP HIS EYES ON HIS FUTURE RATHER THAN HIS PAST.

"Forget the former things; do not dwell on the past. See, I am doing a new thing! Now it springs up; do you not perceive it?" (Isaiah 43:18)

"But one thing I do: Forgetting what is behind and straining toward what is ahead, I press on toward the goal to win the prize for which God has called me heavenward in Christ Jesus." (Philippians 3:13-14)

➤ IF A HUSBAND IS DISAPPOINTED, IT'S BECAUSE HIS HOPE IS IN THE WRONG PLACE.

"..Those who hope in me will not be disappointed." (Isaiah 49:23)

➤ THE HUSBAND MAY OCCASIONALLY FEEL LIKE ALL HIS HARD WORK HAS AMOUNTED TO NOTHING.

"He said to me, "You are my servant, Israel, in whom I will display my splendor." But I said, "I have labored to no purpose; I have spent my strength in vain and for nothing. Yet what is due me is in the LORD's hand, and my reward is with my God. " (Isaiah 49:3-4)

<u>Godly Husband's Notes on Isaiah 49:3-4</u> - It's natural for the godly husband to sometimes feel like his efforts are unappreciated. In Isaiah 49:3, The Father says to His servant (Jesus), "You are my servant, Israel, in whom I will display my splendor." To this, the servant (Jesus) responds to The Father by saying, "I have labored to no purpose; I have spent my strength in vain and for nothing." In this situation, The Father is clearly complimenting His servant's work, but at the same time the servant still feels as if all his hard work and effort has been done to no avail. Now if the ultimate servant, "Jesus Christ" felt this way at times, why wouldn't the godly husband feel this way at times as well? It's bound to happen. But the godly husband must never let feelings of futility cripple his walk with God. He should instead focus on the second half the servant's statement in Isaiah 49:4, which says, "<u>Yet</u> what is due me is in the LORD's hand, and my reward is with my God." Despite his feelings of futility, the servant puts the matter back in the Lord's hands where it belongs. This scripture is eerily similar to Matt 26:39 where the servant (Jesus) says, "Father if it is possible, may this cup be taken from me. <u>Yet</u> not what I will but what you will." Here again is another situation where a servant's feelings come to challenge the will of God. But in the end its God's will that prevails. The godly husband should think about this scripture whenever feelings of doubt and futility invite him to deter him from submission to the will of God.

➢ **A HUSBAND CANNOT SERVE BOTH GOD AND IDOLS.**

"They worshiped the LORD, but they also served their own gods in accordance with the customs of the nations from which they had been brought." (2 Kings 17:33)

"They would not listen, however, but persisted in their former practices. <u>Even while these people were worshiping the LORD, they were serving their idols.</u> To this day their children and grandchildren continue to do so." (2 Kings 17: 40-41)

> ## THE WORD OF GOD IS THE HUSBAND'S COUNSEL.

Your statutes are my delight; they are my counselors. (Psalm 119:24)

> ## THE SERVANT HUSBAND MUST MAKE SURE THAT NEITHER HIS HOME NOR HIS CHURCH IS NEGLECTED.

"I also learned that the portions assigned to the Levites had not been given to them, and that all <u>the Levites and singers responsible for the service had gone back to their own fields</u>. So I rebuked the officials and asked them, "<u>Why is the house of God neglected?</u>" Then I called them together and stationed them at their posts." (Nehemiah 13:10-11)

> ## THE HUSBAND MUST LOVE PRAISE FROM GOD MORE THAN HE LOVES PRAISE FROM PEOPLE.

"....for they loved praise from men more than praise from God." (John 12:43)

> ## GOD WILL REVEAL THE LIFE PATH FOR THE HUSBAND.

"You have made known to me the paths of life...."
(Acts 2:28)

> ## A HUSBAND'S SIN SEPARATES HIM FROM GOD; IT DOES NOT SEPARATE GOD FROM HIM.

"Surely the arm of the lord is not too short to save. Nor his ear to dull to save. But your iniquities have separated you from your God. Your sins have hidden his face from you so that he will not hear." (Isaiah 59:1)

Godly Husband's Notes on Isaiah 59:1 It's not that God is incapable of delivering the husband from his plight. Nor is it that God cannot hear the husband. But rather, the husband's sin is separating him from God. When a husband sins, he spiritually distances himself away from God, even though God still remains close to him. Whenever a husband feels as if God is far away from him, he should first check to see whether his own sin is distancing him from God. God will never leave nor forsake the husband, even if the husband chooses to leave and forsake God. God still remains within the husband's reach at all times.

> ## RECOGNIZING THE VOICE OF GOD IS A SIGN OF A HUSBAND'S FAMILIARITY WITH GOD.

"Again the LORD called, "Samuel!" And Samuel got up and went to Eli and said, "Here I am; you called me." "My son," Eli said, "I did not call; go back and lie down." Now Samuel did not yet know the LORD. The word of the LORD had not yet been revealed to him." (1 Samuel 3:6-7)

Godly Husband's Notes on 1 Samuel 3:6-7 - Samuel failed to respond to the Lord, not because he did not hear the Lord's voice, but because he was not familiar with the Lord's voice. That's the process of getting to know God; recognizing his voice. The more the godly husband gets to know His voice, the more familiar he becomes in his relationship with Him.

> ## A HUSBAND SHOULD NOT LET OTHERS DISTRACT HIM FROM THE VOICE OF GOD.

"When David was told, 'Look, the Philistines are fighting against Keilah and are looting the threshing floors,' he inquired of the LORD, saying, "Shall I go and attack these Philistines?' The

LORD answered him, '**Go**, attack the Philistines and save Keilah.' But David's men said to him, 'Here in Judah we are afraid. How much more, then, if we go to Keilah against the Philistine forces!' Once again David inquired of the LORD , and the LORD answered him, '**Go** down to Keilah, for I am going to give the Philistines into your hand.' So David and his men went to Keilah, fought the Philistines and carried off their livestock. He inflicted heavy losses on the Philistines and saved the people of Keilah." (1 Samuel 23:1-5)

Godly Husband's Notes on 1 Samuel 23:1-5 David wasn't completely sure whether or not he and his men should be assisting the people of Keilah in their fight against the Philistines. So he asked the Lord about it, and the Lord told him to go ahead and help the people of Keilah. But afterwards, David's men reminded him that they were already running scared from Saul and in no position to pick an unprovoked confrontation with the intimidating Philistines. This caused David to re-think whether or not he should do what the Lord instructed. Stuck between two opposing paths, David was compelled to again ask the Lord if he should go. The Lord once again confirmed, "Go down to Keilah, for I am going to give the Philistines into your hand." And based on this second confirmation from the Lord, David went ahead and pursued the Philistines. And as promised, God handed the Philistines into David's hands.

How many times has something like that happened to you? You receive a word from the Lord, and then someone suddenly says something that makes you totally rethink what the Lord just told you. It happens to all of us. But in this situation, rather than following his own fears, or the fears of those around him,

David sought the Lord once again. And again, the Lord affirmed His answer. The more I read about David, the more I understand why the bible calls him "a man after God's own heart."

> **A HUSBAND SHOULD NOT FOLLOW AN INDIVIDUAL JUST BECAUSE THEY CLAIM TO HEAR FROM GOD.**

"So the prophet said to him, 'Come home with me and eat.' The man of God said, 'I cannot turn back and go with you, nor can I eat bread or drink water with you in this place. I have been told by the word of the LORD: 'You must not eat bread or drink water there or return by the way you came.' 'The old prophet answered, 'I too am a prophet, as you are. And an angel said to me by the word of the LORD: 'Bring him back with you to your house so that he may eat bread and drink water.' (But he was lying to him.) So the man of God returned with him and ate and drank in his house." (1 Kings 13:15-19)

Godly Husband's Notes on 1 Kings 13:15-19 In this story, the Lord clearly instructs the man of God to go to his appointed destination without stopping for anything or anyone along the way. But as the man of God began his journey, he came across a man who claimed to be a prophet. After a brief dialogue between the two, the prophet invited the man of God to his home for a meal. He validated his invitation by telling the man of God, "I too am a prophet, as you are." The man of God fell for the prophet's act of deception and went to eat with him at his home. In the end, his disobedience led to his death.

The lesson here for the godly husband is that he should never take advice from someone simply because they claim to have heard from God. Any words that a person speaks on behalf of God, must first: (a) agree with The Word of God itself, and (b) agree with the Word "from God" that's already been impressed on the godly husband's heart. If someone approaches the godly husband and tells him that they've heard from God, but those words do not pass these two vital tests, the husband must reject him.

➢ **WHEN A HUSBAND ASKS THE LORD FOR SOMETHING, HE MUST EXAMINE HIS PERSONAL MOTIVES.**

"You want something but don't get it. You kill and covet, but you cannot have what you want. You quarrel and fight. You do not have, because you do not ask God. When you ask, you do not receive, because you ask with wrong motives, that you may spend what you get on your pleasures". (James 4:2-3)

"Put me on trial, LORD, and cross-examine me. Test my motives and affections." (Psalm 26:2 - NLT)

Godly Husband's Notes on James 4:2-3 "Lord, please give ten million dollars so that I can help the poor!" "Lord, please give me a house so that I can shelter the homeless!" "Lord, please give me a car so that I can help those without transportation!" Why wouldn't God want to answer wonderful prayers like these? Well, it's not that God doesn't want to answer these types of prayers (because He does for many people all around the world each and every day). The problem is, God is not focused on answering your prayer. Answering your prayer is the easy part. God is focused on your growth and development in Him. And part of that growth and development involves your ability to recognize your own true motives for seeking His blessings. God is more concerned about helping you understand what's motivating your request, than he is about fulfilling your request. God challenges us to consider whether or not we're truly being honest with ourselves when we ask Him for things like ten million dollars, a home, or a car. Are we truly asking for these things so that we can benefit others first? Or are we asking for these things so that <u>we can first benefit ourselves</u>? Sure, a person may give away large sums of money to others if they become rich. But who's the first beneficiary?

James 4:2-3 tells us that the real reason people ask God for money is to spend <u>"first"</u> on their own individual pleasures (ouch!). Please keep in mind, spending millions of dollars on oneself is not a sin. However it's a far cry from asking for millions of dollars just to give it away to those in need. The bible is simply calling "a spade a spade," in that "we" want to be the first beneficiary of that money, or that house, or that car because we have the DNA of self-centeredness. With that said, it's very important that the husband deal with his heart first before asking the Lord for anything. He must realize that his selfish desires will always rival the will of the Lord. He must submit his heart and his mind to the Lord on a daily basis, seeking his will in each and every thing that he does. As these traits become embedded within the godly husband's life, you can be sure that anything he asks for will be granted to him.

➢ **<u>A HUSBAND SHOULD ALWAYS BE READY TO GIVE BACK THE VERY THING HE'S ASKED FOR FROM GOD.</u>**

"So in the course of time Hannah conceived and gave birth to a son. <u>She named him Samuel, saying, 'Because I asked the</u>

LORD for him.' When the man Elkanah went up with all his family to offer the annual sacrifice to the LORD and to fulfill his vow, Hannah did not go. She said to her husband, 'After the boy is weaned, I will take him and present him before the LORD, and he will live there always.'"(1 Samuel 2:20-22)

Husband's Notes on 1 Samuel 2:20-22 - Hannah is willing to give back to the Lord the very thing that she prayed and longed for; a son. This is a prototype for the type of relationship that a godly husband must have with the Lord. He must be willing to give up the very thing that he desires most in order to make the Lord his first priority.

> ### A HUSBAND'S HEART CONDITION IMPACTS HIS PRAYERS.

"If I had cherished sin in my heart, the Lord would not have listened; but God has surely listened and heard my voice in prayer. Praise be to God, who has not rejected my prayer or withheld his love from me!" (Psalm 66:18-20)

> ### A HUSBAND'S WIFE TREATMENT IMPACTS HIS PRAYERS.

"In the same way, you husbands must give honor to your wives. Treat your wife with understanding as you live together. She may be weaker than you are, but she is your equal partner in God's gift of new life. Treat her as you should so your prayers will not be hindered." (1 Peter 3:7 - NLT)

> ### A HUSBAND SHOULDN'T THINK IT'S "GOD'S WILL" JUST BECAUSE SOMETHING THAT HE WANTS COMES TO HIM.

"Saul was told that David had gone to Keilah, and he said, 'God has handed him over to me, for David has imprisoned himself by entering a town with gates and bars.' And Saul called up all his forces for battle, to go down to Keilah to besiege David and his men." (1 Samuel 23:7-8)

<u>Godly Husband's Notes on 1 Samuel 23:7-8</u> - Saul was trying to kill David. He diligently pursued him from place to place, but somehow always managed to miss him. But one day, through no apparent effort of his own, David fell right into the hands of Saul. Due to the relative ease with which this occurred, Saul automatically assumed that it was God's will, and that God had "handed David over to him." Actually, Saul was partially correct. It was God's will, but God wasn't handing David over to Saul. He was doing the exact opposite. He was handing Saul over to David.

The godly husband will go through similar types of experiences, where something that he really wants comes to him without any effort. And without hesitation, his tendency will be to grab that thing and convince himself that the Lord wanted him to have it. He may even take the opportunity to call himself "blessed and highly favored!" But does this necessarily mean that God wanted the husband to have that particular thing? It's possible that he handed it over to him just to test his ability to restrain himself (as he did with Solomon). Or maybe He gave it to him to see if he would be willing to give that thing back to Him (as he did with Hannah). Or maybe he didn't want him to have it all, but gave it to him out of his persistence (as he did with the people of Israel when they asked for a King). Just because something "comes to" the godly husband, does not mean that God wants him to have it. The godly husband must consult the Lord for direction before consulting his appetite.

<u>More Godly Husband's Notes on 1 Samuel 23:7-8</u> - I remember speaking to a husband who told me that he was not getting much attention at all from his wife. He said that he had

struggled with infidelity in the past, and his wife was still having a hard time forgiving him. And after enduring what the husband believed to be "an elongated period of rejection" he once again began availing himself to the petitions of other women. And one day, through no apparent effort of his own, the husband came across a woman who really enjoyed giving him attention. Immediately, the first thing that came to his mind was, "Praise the Lord! God sent me a woman who cares about my needs!" His desire for emotional fulfillment became the lens through which he interpreted the will of God. He wanted emotional fulfillment, and emotional fulfillment showed up at his door, so obviously it had to be God's will for him. When a husband makes assumptions like this without taking the time to seek the Lord and understand what's governing his own heart, he will undoubtedly make fatal errors in judgment. A husband cannot assume it's the will of God just because something that he wants comes to him without effort. He must still search the heart of God, while at the same time searching his own heart.

> ## A HUSBAND MUST NEVER BLAME GOD FOR HIS TEMPTATIONS, AFFLICTIONS OR MISFORTUNES.

"The LORD has afflicted me; the Almighty has brought misfortune upon me." (Ruth 1:21)

"When tempted, no one should say, "God is tempting me. For God cannot be tempted by evil, nor does he tempt anyone; but each person is tempted when they are dragged away by their own evil desire and enticed." (James 1:13-15)

> ## THERE ARE CONSEQUENCES WHEN A HUSBAND COMMITS TO A LIFE OF PROMISCUITY.

"Since you have forgotten me and thrust me behind your back, you must bear the consequences of your lewdness and prostitution." (Ezekiel 23:35)

> ## WHEN A HUSBAND REPEATEDLY ABANDONS THE LORD IN PURSUIT OF OTHER THINGS, GOD WILL EVENTUALLY GIVE HIM OVER TO THOSE THINGS.

"But my people would not listen to me; Israel would not submit to me. So I gave them over to their stubborn hearts to follow their own devices. If my people would but listen to me, if Israel would follow my ways, how quickly would I subdue their enemies and turn my hand against their foes!" (Psalm 81:11-14)

> ## THE HUSBAND SHOULD NOT ATTEMPT TO RATIONALIZE HIS DISOBEDIENCE.

"Will you steal and murder, commit adultery and perjury, burn incense to Baal and follow other gods you have not known, and then come and stand before me in this house, which bears my Name, and say, "We are safe"- safe to do all these detestable things?" (Jeremiah 7:9-11)

When such a person hears the words of this oath, he invokes a blessing on himself and therefore thinks, "I will be safe, even though I persist in going my own way."(Deuteronomy 29:19)

Husband's Notes on Deuteronomy 29:19 - There will be times when a godly husband disobeys the Lord, yet still declares a blessing upon his disobedience. "I will be safe, even though I persist in going my own way" the husband says. It's amazing, but we declare blessings over our disobedience each and every day. When the diabetic says "I'll just have one little slice of cake, I'll be o.k." he declares a blessing upon himself despite his poor dietary choices. When a man buys something with a credit card, without having the money to pay for it, he declares a blessing upon himself despite his poor financial decision. He's essentially saying, "I'll still be ok even though I cannot afford this." **A self-invoked blessing is only as good as its source of endorsement**. So if fleshly desires are the endorser of your blessings, then your blessings will prosper to the degree that your flesh prospers.

More Husband's Notes on Deuteronomy 29:19 - There are some married men who choose to live lives of promiscuity. They participate in practices that defile both their relationship with God and the marriage covenant. They live adulterous lives, while at the same time telling themselves, "I will be safe, even though I persist in going my own way." And despite the potential health ramifications of their reckless actions, they indulge themselves again and again. This is the life of a man who rationalizes his sin.

> ## THE HUSBAND SHOULD VIEW HIS AFFLICTIONS IN A POSITIVE LIGHT.

"It was good for me to be afflicted so that I might learn your decrees." (Psalm 119:71)

> ## THE SAME GOD WHO PERMITS INJURY TO THE HUSBAND, IS THE SAME GOD WHO HEALS THE HUSBAND.

"For he wounds, but he also binds up; he injures, but his hands also heal." (Job 5:17-18)

> ## A HUSBAND CANNOT COME BEFORE THE LORD EMPTY-HANDED.

"No one is to appear before me empty-handed."
(Exodus 23:15)

➤ IT IS GOD WHO BEARS THE HUSBAND'S BURDENS ON A DAILY BASIS.

"Praise be to the Lord, to God our Savior, who daily bears our burdens. Selah." (Psalm 68:19)

➤ THE HOLY SPIRIT SERVES AS BOTH A TEACHER AND A REMINDER FOR HUSBANDS.

"But the Counselor, the Holy Spirit, whom the Father will send in my name, will teach you all things and will remind you of everything I have said to you." (John 14:26)

➤ A HUSBAND NEED NOT BOAST ABOUT HIS FUTURE.

"Now listen, you who say, 'Today or tomorrow we will go to this or that city, spend a year there, carry on business and make money.' Why, you do not even know what will happen tomorrow. What is your life? You are a mist that appears for a little while and then vanishes. Instead, you ought to say, "If it is the Lord's will, we will live and do this or that. As it is, you boast and brag. All such boasting is evil." (James 4:13-16)

➤ IF A WIFE ACCIDENTALLY HURTS OR OFFENDS HER HUSBAND, THAT HUSBAND SHOULD OFFER HIS WIFE A CITY OF REFUGE.

"Then the LORD said to Joshua: 'Tell the Israelites to designate the cities of refuge, as I instructed you through Moses, so that anyone who kills a person accidentally and unintentionally may flee there and find protection from the avenger of blood." (Joshua 20:1-3)

Husband's Notes on Joshua 20:1-3 - In the Old Testament, God established what was called, "a city of refuge." This was a place where a person could go if they accidentally committed a crime or wronged another individual (or their property). This was a place that protected the offender and kept them free from harm while the victim and/or family members healed from their emotional, physical and psychological wounds.

Husbands should think about this "city of refuge" concept, and how it may at times prove valuable in his marriage relationship. Naturally, there will be times in a marriage where a wife unintentionally says or does something to hurt her husband's feelings. When this happens, it's incumbent upon him to create a safe place for her to go as he works through his hurt feelings. He must find a way to give her a "city of refuge."

➢ **WHEN A WISE HUSBAND STUMBLES, IT IS FOR HIS OWN REFINEMENT AND PURIFICATION.**

"Some of the wise will stumble, so that they may be refined, purified and made spotless until the time of the end, for it will still come at the appointed time." (Daniel 11:35)

➢ **A HUSBAND MUST REMAIN TRUE TO HIS GOD-GIVEN PURPOSE RATHER THAN CHASING FAME, RECOGNITION, OR POWER.**

"Once the trees searched for someone to be king; they asked the olive tree, 'Will you be our king?' But the olive tree replied, 'My oil brings honor to people and gods. I won't stop making oil, just to have my branches wave above the other trees.' Then they asked the fig tree, 'Will you be our king?' But the fig tree replied, 'I won't stop growing my delicious fruit, just to have my branches wave above the other trees.' Next they asked the grape vine, 'Will you be our king?' But the grape vine replied, 'My wine brings cheer to people and gods. I won't stop making wine, just to have my branches wave above the other trees.'" (Judges 9:8-13 – CEV)

Husband's Note on Judges 9:8-13   The essential idea here is that the olive tree, fig tree, and grape vine all were invited to walk away from their unique, god-given purpose to pursue a life of kingship over all the other trees. This meant that they would be the largest of all trees, and have their branches wave far above the others. But the olive tree, fig tree, and grape vine each believed that departing from their purpose simply so that they could be above everyone else wasn't worth it. They were more content in expressing the unique function that God called them to. This is a great pattern for the godly husband to follow. He should never make decisions based on how much fame, recognition or power he'll receive. He should instead make decisions based on what it is God is calling him to do. The olive tree, fig tree, and grape vine were all wise enough to reject the more prestigious offer that was presented to them. The godly husband must be equally as wise.

> ### THE ONLY SACRIFICE GOD WANTS FROM A HUSBAND IS HIS BROKENNESS.

"You do not delight in sacrifice, or I would bring it; you do not take pleasure in burnt offerings. The sacrifices of God are a broken spirit; a broken and contrite heart, O God, you will not despise." (Psalm 51:15-17)

> ### A HUSBAND MUST DECIDE WHETHER HE WILL FORGIVE SINS, OR RETAIN SINS.

"If you forgive the sins of any, their sins have been forgiven them; if you retain the sins of any, they have been retained."

201

(John 20:23 - NASB)

<u>Husband's Notes on John 20:22-23</u>: When a husband is sinned against, he will either become a sin retainer, or sin forgiver. If he becomes a sin forgiver, he releases himself and his offenders from their transgressions against him. If he becomes a sin retainer, he ends up confining himself and his transgressors to the sins that perpetrated against him. The godly husband must decide whether he's going to be a sin retainer or sin forgiver. He must decide whether he will engage the practice of releasing others or imprisoning himself.

Chapter 10

A Husband's Notes

Biblical References For The Godly Husband

Traits of a Husband's Wisdom:

(James 3:17)

1. Pure
2. Peace-loving
3. Full of mercy
4. Good fruit
5. Impartial
6. Sincere

Benefits of a Husband's Wisdom:

1. Valuable/Precious (Proverbs 6:15)
2. Incomparable (Proverbs 3:15)
3. Long Lasting and Prosperous (Proverbs 3:16)
4. Pleasant (Proverbs 3:17)
5. Peaceful (Proverbs 3:17)

Benefits of a Husband's Patience:

1. Fosters Understanding (Proverbs 14:29)
2. Calms Contentions (Proverbs 15:18)
3. Influences Leadership (Proverbs 25:15)

Traits of a Husband's Love:

(I Corinthians 13:4)

1. He is patient with his wife
2. He is kind to his wife
3. He does not envy his wife
4. He does not boast unto his wife
5. He is not proud unto his wife
6. He is not rude unto his wife
7. He is not self-seeking before his wife
8. He is not easily angered before his wife
9. He keeps no record of wrongs against his wife
10. He does not delight in evil against his wife, but rejoices in telling his wife the truth
11. He always protects his wife
12. He always trusts with her
13. He always hopes with her
14. He always perseveres with her

Signs of A Husband's Spiritual Maturity:

(Galatians 5:22)

1. His Love towards his wife
2. His Joy towards his wife
3. His Peace towards his wife
4. His Patience towards his wife
5. His Goodness towards his wife
6. HIs Gentleness towards his wife
7. His Faithfulness towards his wife
8. HIs Kindness towards his wife
9. His Self-Control towards his wife

How the Husband Lives A Blameless Life:
(Psalm 101)

1. By living a life of integrity in his home (Psalm 101:2)
2. By protecting his eyes (Psalm 101:3)
3. By protecting his heart (Psalm 101:4)
4. By separating himself from sin (Psalm 101:4)
5. By refraining from negative talk against others (Psalm 101:5)
6. By avoiding pride (Psalm 101:5)
7. By ministering to God within his daily walk (Psalm 101:6)
8. By being transparent, honest and truthful (Psalm 101:7)
9. By cutting off all unrighteous relationships (Psalm 101:8)

What Type of Husband Does the Lord Wish to Dwell With?
(Isaiah 33:15)

1. A husband who walks righteously
2. A husband who speaks righteously
3. A husband who rejects illegal gain
4. A husband who keeps his hand from accepting gifts in exchange for favors
5. A husband who protects his ears from gossip & slanderous talk.
6. A husband who guards his eyes

How a Husband Returns to the Lord With all His Heart:
(1 Samuel 7:2-3)

1. By rededicating himself to the Lord
2. By ridding himself of compromising influences
3. By serving no other Gods except The Lord

Developmental Tips For The Godly Husband

5 Steps to Change in a Husband's Life:

1. Identify his wrong (see it)
2. Confess his wrong (speak it)
3. Own his wrong (take it)
4. Repent of his wrong (release it)
5. Turn from his wrong (leave it)

How a Husband Takes Full Responsibility:

1. By Making Himself Accountable (owning the answer)
2. By Making Himself Culpable (owning the wrongdoing)
3. By Making Himself Liable (owning the blame)

Seven Ways That a Husband Connects With His Wife:

1. Through Spoken Word
2. Through Written Word
3. Through Thoughts
4. Through Prayers
5. Through Eye Contact
6. Through Physical Contact
7. Through Facial and/or Bodily Gestures

4 Motivations for a Husband's Obedience:

1. Force (He has to do it)
2. Necessity (He needs to do it)
3. Desire (He wants to do it)
4. Love (He wills to do it)

The 5 Steps of Fruit-Bearing Within a Husband's Life:

1. His Spirit Gives Birth To His Desires

2. HIs Desires Give Birth To His Intentions

3. HIs Intensions Give Birth To His Commitments

4. HIs Commitments Give Birth To His Actions

5. HIs Actions Give Birth To His Fruit

6 Aspects of a Husband's Competency:

1. His **Perception**: Does he perceive things and people around him?

2. His **Memory**: Does he remember things that he's told?

3. His **Sincerity**: Is he genuine in his actions?

4. His **Ability to Communicate**: Does he express himself well?

5. His **Trustworthiness**: Can he be trusted?

6. His **Knowledge**: How knowledgeable is he?

Seven Things That Cause Mood Swings Within the Husband:

1. Physical changes (i.e. weight, health, appearance, etc.)

2. Hormonal/chemical imbalances

3. Negative Work life/Work Overload

4. Negative home life

5. Unmet Commitments (bills, chores, cleaning, children, etc.)

6. Untimely or insensitive statements made by others

7. Internal conflicts (unresolved issues with friends, family, etc.)

The Husband's Testimony is Comprised of 3 things:

1. His **Witness of Truth** - The ability to identify the truth

2. His **Communication of Truth**- The ability to speak the truth

3. His **Evidence of Truth** – The ability to live the truth

The Husband's "Big Seven":

1- Faith

2- Love

3- Trust

4- Communication

5- Intimacy

6- Patience

7- Wisdom (godly)

A Godly Husband's Final Thought

"The Husband who depends upon the Holy Spirit to guide his conversation is like a soldier armed with an arsenal of weaponry. He knows war to be an inevitability rather than a mere possibility. He knows the intricacies of each weapon, as he knows himself. He understands the critical nature of execution, for his life depends upon it. He understands the proper weapon to be used in each individual battle, as well as the degree of force to be applied."

If you have an inquiry or testimonial to share about "Inside the Mind of a Godly Husband" please forward to: Gene@insidethemindofagodlyhusband.com.

Thank You!